THE SIMPLE KITCHEN

QUICK AND EASY RECIPES BURSTING WITH FLAVOR

CHAD AND **DONNA ELICK**

CREATORS OF
THE HUGELY POPULAR
COOKING WEBSITE

THE
SLOW ROASTED
ITALIAN

PAGE STREET
PUBLISHING CO.

PAGE STREET
PUBLISHING CO.

First published in 2017 by
Page Street Publishing Co.
27 Congress Street, Suite 105
Salem, MA 01970
www.pagestreetpublishing.com

Distributed by Macmillan, sales in Canada by The Canadian Manda Group.

22 21 20 19 18   2 3 4 5 6

ISBN-13: 978-1-62414-435-6
ISBN-10: 1-62414-435-7

Library of Congress Control Number: 2017935277
Cover photo and design by Chad A. Elick

Book design by Page Street Publishing Co.
Photography by Chad Elick

Printed and bound in the United States

For Sierra,

You always give us something to look forward to and make every day the *best day ever*. Your wonderful spirit inspires us and you fill our lives with love, laughter and sparkles!

CONTENTS

INTRO

Welcome to *The Simple Kitchen*! We are Donna and Chad Elick, the creators of the cooking website and blog The Slow Roasted Italian. Over the years, we've developed and photographed more than 1,000 recipes for the millions of readers who come to our site looking for tasty time-saving solutions. We've learned how to turn recipes that traditionally take a long time to cook into quick and easy dishes that are bursting with flavor and made with as many real ingredients as possible.

I'm Donna, the storyteller in the family. Allow me to guide you through our delicious recipes in this book; my amazing husband, Chad, will handle the show-and-tell with mouthwatering photography! As a young adult living on my own, I enjoyed cooking the meals that my mom taught me and found that it brought me great joy to feed people. Cooking for Chad for the first time, I proudly served him frozen chicken fried steak and boxed mashed potatoes. Thank goodness he stuck around after that. Lucky for Chad, it *really* worked out!

It's funny to think that the path to writing this book all started with a recipe that my mom shared with me years ago. One day, my mom called to tell me about a dessert she had had at work. She insisted I make it, and let me tell you—those pecan squares were amazing! Shortly after that, while flipping through the channels, I landed on Ina Garten making the same recipe that my mom had given me. I stopped, remembering how delicious they were. So, I watched and learned. Passion was ignited in me to get into the kitchen and try new things with Chad by my side coming up with delicious ideas.

Before long, our family and friends were asking for recipes for our newest creations. Chad and I decided to put them online, so everyone we knew could find them. In the summer of 2011, The Slow Roasted Italian was born. If you know anything about us, you know that Chad and I are like Frick and Frack, partners in love and life, and you can't find one of us without the other. Naturally, Chad was right there, camera in hand. He has an incredible knack for making our recipes look as delicious as they taste, dontchathink? Chad is the amazing photographer and designer for our popular website. He's also the mastermind behind the food fusion recipes that we create for you. Hello, delicious!

After our daughter, Sierra, was born, everything in life changed. Making smarter food choices really became a priority. Plus, I wanted to spend time with my family, not in the kitchen cooking. So my love of all day cooking transformed into a passion for creating quick and easy recipes made with real ingredients that are full of flavor.

Our recipes are inspired by our lives, the places we have lived and the food we have enjoyed in our travels. We love to find ways to take a complicated recipe and make it simply, without sacrificing flavor. Our recipes taste so good that an hour later you are still thinking, "Dang, that was some good food. I can't wait to eat it again!"

Among our recipes, you will find Mexican flavors, like our Mexican Roast Beef Dip (page 25); Italian food, such as our Three-Cheese Meat Lasagna (page 10) and Tuscan Garlic Chicken and Linguine (page 56); Midwestern recipes, such as Hearty Beef Soup (page 99) and Down-Home Pot Roast with Carrots and Potatoes (page 13); and Southern food, including Crispy Southern Fried Chicken (page 81), Triple Cheesy Mac and Cheese (page 14) and so much more.

We are absolutely giddy that you have picked up this book, and we look forward to hearing all about the delicious meals you have created! We have included more than 80 scrumptious recipes, with a handful of family favorites from our website that we just had to share with you. We hope that our recipes inspire you to cook simply and, of course, share!

With love,
Donna
&
Chad
xxxooo

ONE

PERFECTLY SLOW-COOKED

Recipes that are so easy they just about cook themselves are an integral tool in our simple kitchen, so much so that the slow cooker recipes overflowed from this chapter into other sections. Be sure to look for more slow cooker recipes throughout the book. I have a bit of a slow cooker "thing."

I really embraced my slow cooker after my daughter was born. All of a sudden, I found I wanted to spend less time in the kitchen and more time with my family. At the time, I had one small round slow cooker that I bought when I moved out on my own. Many years later, I now have eight of them. Obsess much? Yes! I am totally in love with the "set it and forget it" way of cooking. These recipes are so easy that we have tagged each one with how long the prep work takes, because the slow cooker does the rest of the work.

Our recipes are inspired by where we have lived and the food our families have experienced.

I grew up on the sandy beaches of a small town in southwest Florida, where the sun and the sand were everything. Southern food melted my heart, and in the end, it became a delicious influence in our kitchen and our recipes. Now we crave it! Our finger lickin' good Melt-in-Your-Mouth Spicy Sweet Ribs (page 21) and Kickin' Southern-Style Pulled Pork (page 17) are Southern staples, and now they can be made right in your slow cooker.

Chad was born and raised in America's Heartland. My meat-and-potato-loving husband is an Iowan through and through, so the Down-Home Pot Roast with Carrots and Potatoes (page 13) really rocks his world!

When I was in my twenties I met the man of my dreams (yes, of course, it was Chad, silly!) and he lived across the country, so I loaded up the truck and moved to Phoenix . . . Arizona, that is . . . where I found an abundance of flavors that I had no idea existed, and now they are nearly a part of my DNA, such as our Mexican Roast Beef Dip Sandwich (page 25). It's a play on the ever-popular French dip with a delicious Mexican twist.

Triple Cheesy Mac and Cheese (page 14) is quite possibly our daughter's favorite recipe in this book. This recipe is so gratifying I literally broke out into my happy dance with a chorus of ummmms following behind me. It's rich and creamy, utterly cheesy and perfectly worthy of a special occasion!

This chapter wouldn't be complete without a recipe inspired by my Italian roots. We ate a lot of New York–style Italian food when I was growing up: lots of pasta and cheese. Obviously, the love of cheese really stuck. Three-Cheese Meat Lasagna is our favorite lasagna ever, and it's going to light up your palate (page 10).

So, what are you waiting for? Grab your slow cooker and let's get cookin'.

THREE-CHEESE MEAT LASAGNA

Growing up Italian, I ate a lot of traditional Italian food, and lasagna was always my favorite. So, it's no surprise that Chad and I have tried lasagna at restaurants all over the country. But none of them really hit the mark. Finally, we created a lasagna recipe that we love, love, love! This Three-Cheese Meat Lasagna has the perfect amount of heat to light up your taste buds. We just can't get enough of it. It's a scrumptious recipe that comes together in just about 15 minutes and has layer after layer of flavorful hot Italian sausage, spicy tomato sauce, pasta and three ooey-gooey cheeses! I mean, can you really ever have enough cheese?

2 lb (908 g) hot Italian sausage, casings removed

2 recipes 10-Minute Marinara Arrabbiata (page 147), blended

1 cup (235 ml) water

1 (32-oz [908-g]) container part-skim ricotta cheese

2 large eggs, beaten

1 tsp kosher salt

1 tsp freshly ground pepper

20 fresh basil leaves, chiffonade, divided

2 cups (200 g) freshly shredded Parmesan cheese, divided

3 cups (360 g) freshly shredded mozzarella cheese, divided

16 oven-ready lasagna noodles

In a 12-inch (30.5-cm) skillet over medium-high heat, cook the sausage until browned and cooked through, 5 to 7 minutes. Break up the sausage with a spatula as it cooks. Drain the excess drippings if necessary. Pour the marinara and water into the skillet with the cooked sausage and simmer for 5 minutes, stirring occasionally. Remove from the heat.

Meanwhile, in a medium bowl, combine the ricotta, eggs, salt, pepper and half of the chiffonaded basil leaves. Stir until completely blended. Add 1 cup (100 g) of the Parmesan cheese and 2 cups (240 g) of the mozzarella. Stir to combine.

Spray a 6-quart (6-L) slow cooker with nonstick cooking spray. Spread 2 cups (480 g) of sauce onto the bottom of the slow cooker. Top with a layer of noodles, breaking them to fit (about 4 noodles). Dollop one-third of the cheese mixture (about 1½ cups [360 g]) and smooth it into an even layer with a spatula. Spread 2 cups (480 g) of meat sauce over the cheese. Repeat to make two more layers of noodles, cheese mixture, sauce, noodles, cheese mixture and sauce. Add a fourth layer of noodles, spread the remaining sauce over the top and sprinkle the remaining 1 cup (120 g) of mozzarella on top.

Cover and cook for 2½ to 3 hours on high (or 5 to 6 hours on low), until the pasta is al dente (has a bite to it). Turn off the slow cooker and let stand for 20 to 30 minutes before serving. This will help the lasagna cool and will make cutting much easier. Top with the remaining 1 cup (100 g) of Parmesan cheese and the remaining chiffonaded basil leaves.

DONNA'S SIMPLE KITCHEN TIP: You can prepare this same recipe in a lasagna pan, divided into three layers instead of four. Cover and bake in a 425°F (220°C, or gas mark 7) oven for 20 minutes. Then uncover and bake for 5 more minutes. Let the lasagna cool at room temperature for 5 to 10 minutes to make it a little easier to cut, if you can wait. We never can!

DOWN-HOME POT ROAST WITH CARROTS AND POTATOES

This pot roast is so tender and juicy that the beef melts in your mouth. It's a simple slow cooker meal with layers of heavenly flavors in a rich, red wine gravy that is loaded with potatoes and carrots. It is truly the ultimate comfort food! This simple recipe takes just 25 minutes of prep time and is sure to be on your table all year long. This is almost like Mom used to make, but better, much better! Sorry, Moms.

3 lb (1.4 kg) boneless beef chuck roast, cut into chunks

1 tbsp (18 g) kosher salt

2 tsp (4 g) coarsely ground black pepper

4 tbsp (60 ml) extra virgin olive oil, divided

1 medium yellow onion, sliced

6 cloves garlic, minced

2 tbsp (6 g) Tuscan-Style Seasoning Blend (page 160)

1 tbsp (15 ml) Worcestershire sauce

1 cup (235 ml) red wine (I used Cabernet Sauvignon)

3 cups (705 ml) low-sodium beef stock

2 cups (240 g) baby carrots

2 lb (908 g) baby red potatoes, cut in half or quarters if large

2 tbsp (16 g) cornstarch

¼ cup (60 ml) water

Cut the beef into 3-inch (7.5-cm) chunks and season with the salt and pepper.

Warm 2 tablespoons (30 ml) of the olive oil in a large Dutch oven (or oven-safe heavy-bottomed pot) over medium-high heat. Once you can feel the heat when you hold your hand 6 inches (15 cm) above the pot, place the roast pieces in the pot. Brown the pieces on all sides, 2 to 3 minutes per side. Don't skip this step. We are adding layers of flavor here. Once the roast is nicely seared with a good crust, remove it from the Dutch oven and place it in your slow cooker. I use my 5-quart (4.5-L) oval cooker for this recipe.

Add the remaining 2 tablespoons (30 ml) of olive oil and the onions to the Dutch oven and cook until the onions are translucent, 3 to 4 minutes. Add the garlic and cook for about 30 seconds. Sprinkle in the seasoning blend and add the Worcestershire sauce. Stir to combine. Pour in the wine. Deglaze the pan by scraping up the browned bits at the bottom of the pan with a wooden spoon or spatula as it bubbles. Pour in the beef stock. Stir to combine, and then add the contents of the pot into the slow cooker. Cover and cook for 5 hours on high (or 10 hours on low). Add the carrots and potatoes halfway through the cook time.

Remove the roast and vegetables from the slow cooker and place them on a serving dish. Tent with foil. Ladle the cooking liquid into a 4-quart (3.6-L) saucepan and bring it to a boil over medium-high heat. Combine the cornstarch and water in a mason jar. Seal and shake the living tar out of it to create a slurry. Pour the slurry into the pot and stir. Boil the gravy until thickened, 3 to 5 minutes. Taste for seasoning, and add salt and pepper as necessary.

Serve the pot roast and veggies with gravy on the side.

DONNA'S SIMPLE KITCHEN TIP: If you are sensitive to alcohol, you can substitute the wine with beef stock or grape, pomegranate or cranberry juice.

TRIPLE CHEESY MAC AND CHEESE

This is truly one of our favorite recipes in this book! It's pure comfort in a bowl, with perfectly tender corkscrew pasta with twists and ridges that capture the luscious pepper Jack and cheddar cheese sauce. It has just enough heat to wake up your taste buds. Everyone devoured it at Thanksgiving dinner this year, and Sierra loves this recipe so much that she asked me, "Mommy, can I make your yummy slow cooker mac and cheese tonight?" How could I say no . . . to someone else cooking dinner? So yes, we now know that this recipe is so easy our seven-year-old can make it! And it's on the weekly meal plan.

1 lb (454 g) cellentani pasta (also known as cavatappi), uncooked

4 tbsp (55 g) unsalted butter, sliced into 1-tbsp (14-g) pieces

4 oz (112 g) cream cheese, cut into 1-oz (28-g) pieces

1 tsp kosher salt

½ tsp cayenne pepper

3 cups (705 ml) whole milk

½ cup (120 ml) heavy cream

2 cups (240 g) freshly shredded sharp cheddar cheese

1 cup (120 g) fresh shredded pepper Jack cheese

Pour the uncooked pasta onto the bottom of your slow cooker. I love my 6-quart (5.4-L) for this recipe. Scatter the butter and cream cheese pieces over the pasta. Sprinkle the salt and cayenne pepper over the top and pour the milk and cream into the slow cooker. Stir to combine everything and smooth the pasta into one even layer coated in sauce.

Cover and cook on low for 1 to 2 hours, until the pasta is chewy (not quite crunchy, but very al dente). Your cook time will vary if you use a different pasta, so start with 1 hour and adjust from there. Stir once halfway through the cook time and be sure to smooth the pasta into one layer so it is well coated with the sauce. Once the pasta is ready, sprinkle on the cheddar and pepper Jack cheeses and stir to combine. The cheese will melt into the sauce to create the most luxurious creamy cheese sauce. Cover the mac and cheese and cook for 10 minutes, until the cheese is melted and it comes together. Stir before serving.

DONNA'S SIMPLE KITCHEN TIP: The cheese sauce will thicken as it cools. If you plan to hold the mac and cheese in the slow cooker on warm, add extra milk as needed to keep the sauce nice and creamy. Also, if you are going to refrigerate it to eat later, add enough milk to the pasta to thin out the sauce before refrigerating. That way when you pull it out, it will scoop easily and the mac and cheese will warm up perfectly in the microwave or on the stove top. We do this every week and portion it out for easy lunches.

KICKIN' SOUTHERN-STYLE PULLED PORK

This is the ultimate tangy pulled pork sandwich with a spicy kick. It's a Southern classic! With layers of flavor built on the perfectly caramelized crusted pork and a zippy brown sugar au jus, it doesn't need any barbecue sauce. It's served on a toasted bun with creamy coleslaw on the side. Chad and I loved this so much we ate every bite. TWICE. The pulled pork is great on a garden salad with ranch dressing, and the leftovers make for amazing nachos! Well, if you have any leftovers.

1 tbsp (6 g) smoked paprika

1 tbsp (6 g) New Mexico chile powder

1 tbsp (6 g) garlic powder

1 tbsp (18 g) kosher salt

1–3 tsp (2–6 g) ground cayenne pepper (to taste)

2 tsp (4 g) black pepper

5 lb (2.3 g) pork shoulder

2 tbsp (30 ml) extra light olive oil

1 cup (235 ml) apple cider vinegar

½ cup (112 g) packed light brown sugar

12 sweet hamburger buns

Coleslaw, for serving (optional)

Combine the paprika, chile powder, garlic powder, salt, cayenne and pepper in a gallon-size (3.6-L) zip-top bag. Seal and shake until everything is combined; set aside.

Rinse the pork under cool water and pat it dry with a paper towel. Place the pork into the bag with the seasoning. Seal and shake the bag until the pork is coated with the spice mixture. It's okay if you have some seasoning left in the bag; save it. We will use that later.

Heat a Dutch oven, or heavy-bottomed pot, over medium-high heat. Once you can feel the heat when you hold your hand 6 inches (15 cm) above the pot, add the olive oil. Carefully place the pork into the hot pot using tongs. Sear each side of the pork until it has a rich brown crust on it. You will need to allow the pork to sizzle in the pan without moving it for at least 2 to 3 minutes per side. Place the pork into your slow cooker. I use my 6-quart (5.4-L) oval.

Place your pot back on the stove over medium-high heat. Carefully add the vinegar to your pot. Stand back a little as you pour it into the hot pot or you will give yourself a vinegar steam facial. Use a spatula to scrape the stuck-on browned bits from the bottom of the pot. Once the mixture is boiling, add the brown sugar and stir until the sugar dissolves. Pour the liquid over the pork in the slow cooker.

Sprinkle the remaining seasoning from the bag over the pork. Cover the slow cooker and cook for 5 to 6 hours on high (or 10 to 12 hours on low). When the pork is tender enough to pull apart easily, use two forks to shred the meat, removing any visible fat. Stir the pork in the sauce. Allow the pork to absorb those yummy juices while you prepare the buns.

Meanwhile, preheat the oven to 425°F (220°C, or gas mark 7). Split the buns and place them on a baking sheet cut side up. Toast them in the oven until the edges are golden brown, 4 to 5 minutes.

Serve a heaping spoonful of pulled pork on your toasted bun. Top with coleslaw, if you like. I prefer mine with slaw on the side.

DONNA'S SIMPLE KITCHEN TIP: Pork shoulder (also known as picnic shoulder or Boston butt) is the perfect cut of pork for this recipe. It is incredibly marbled with fat, making it luscious, tender and the most flavorful cut. Luckily, it is also a very inexpensive cut of meat.

FIESTA CHICKEN STREET TACOS

This fantastic simple recipe is inspired by some awesome food truck eats Chad and I enjoyed while eating our way through Houston. And boy, did we eat. Street tacos are the ultimate convenient walking food, and this slow cooker fiesta chicken is so easy it just about cooks itself. Chunks of tomato, onion and chiles are speckled throughout the perfectly tender and juicy chicken, with sweet corn and black beans bringing it all together. It's piled on a tortilla and topped with all the fixin's your taco can hold.

2 lb (908 g) boneless skinless chicken breasts

1 recipe (2 cups [480 g]) Restaurant-Style Chunky Salsa (page 151)

1 (15-oz [425-g]) can reduced-sodium black beans, drained and rinsed

1 (14.25-oz [400-g]) can niblet corn, drained

2 tbsp (14 g) Mexican Seasoning Blend (page 160)

1 tsp kosher salt

16 small flour tortillas

TOPPINGS

Guacamole

Sliced red onion

Squeeze of lime juice

Chopped fresh cilantro

Crumbled feta or Cotija cheese

Place the chicken breasts on the bottom of the slow cooker. I love my 5-quart (4.5-L) round for this recipe. Pour the salsa, beans, corn, seasoning blend and salt over the chicken. Stir with a spoon to combine.

Cover and cook for 3 to 4 hours on high (or 6 to 8 hours on low). Once the chicken pulls apart easily, use two forks to shred the chicken. Taste for seasoning. Add salt to taste. Mine usually needs just a pinch. Cook for 30 minutes longer to allow the chicken to absorb the flavorful juices.

Layer 2 flour tortillas on top of each other, add a scoop of the fiesta chicken and top with your preferred fixin's.

DONNA'S SIMPLE KITCHEN TIP: To make quick work of shredding chicken, toss it in your stand mixer and process it with the paddle attachment until shredded.

MELT-IN-YOUR-MOUTH SPICY SWEET RIBS

These are quite possibly the best ribs we have ever eaten! They are the perfect blend of sweet and spicy. They are smoky, flavorful and tender, with a sticky, caramelized, glazed exterior. That spicy sweet sauce takes me back to southwest Florida and the barbecues and pig roasts I enjoyed there. This recipe is so easy that I may never cook them on the grill again. Everyone who tried them begged for the recipe, and let's just say that Chad wasn't crazy about sharing. These ribs are so good, you won't mind getting your fingers messy, and don't be surprised if you find your family licking the plate. Ahem . . . Chad.

RIBS

2 tbsp (14 g) Mexican Seasoning Blend (page 160)

1 tbsp (15 g) packed light brown sugar

1 tsp kosher salt

3 lb (1.4 kg) baby back ribs, trimmed

½ cup (120 ml) beer

BARBECUE SAUCE

1 cup (225 g) ketchup

½ cup (112 g) packed light brown sugar

2 tbsp (30 ml) cider vinegar

2 tbsp (14 g) Mexican Seasoning Blend (page 160)

1 tbsp (15 ml) Worcestershire sauce

1½ tsp (8 g) kosher salt

1 tsp freshly cracked black pepper

½ tsp crushed red pepper flakes

Combine the Mexican seasoning, brown sugar and salt in a small bowl. Stir to combine. Make sure the membrane is removed from the back of the ribs. Press the seasoning onto the ribs and set aside.

Pour the beer into the slow cooker. I prefer to use my 6-quart (5.4-L) oval for this recipe. Place the ribs in the slow cooker, thicker end down and meaty side facing out. Cook for 3 hours on high (or 6 hours on low). As soon as the ends of the bones are sticking out from the meat, they should be done.

Meanwhile, to make the sauce, combine the barbecue sauce ingredients in a small saucepan and bring to a boil over medium heat, stirring occasionally, about 5 minutes. Set aside until the ribs are ready.

Preheat your oven to 375°F (190°C, or gas mark 5). Place the ribs on a foil-lined baking sheet. Slather the top and undersides of the ribs with the barbecue sauce. Bake for 10 to 15 minutes, until the sauce caramelizes. Remove from the oven and serve.

DONNA'S SIMPLE KITCHEN TIP: If you are sensitive to alcohol, you can substitute the beer with chicken broth.

LEMON GARLIC CHICKEN THIGHS AND VEGGIES

Browned and slow-cooked, these bone-in chicken thighs create a luxurious base for this amazingly flavorful lemon garlic dish, complete with potatoes and veggies for the ultimate simple chicken dinner the whole family will love. Lemon is one of our favorite flavors; we enjoy it in savory dishes, it's amazing in desserts and I love my share of lemon water and lemonade, all thanks to Juicy Lucy, our abundant lemon tree. Even if you don't have your own Lucy, store-bought lemons are delicious too!

2 lb (908 g) red potatoes, quartered

3 lb (1.4 kg) bone-in, skin-on chicken thighs (about 8 thighs)

4 tsp (4 g) Tuscan-Style Seasoning Blend (page 160)

2 tsp (12 g) kosher salt

2 tsp (6 g) freshly ground black pepper

4 tbsp (60 ml) extra virgin olive oil, divided

6 cloves garlic, minced

1 cup (235 ml) white wine (I used Chardonnay)

2 cups (470 ml) reduced-sodium chicken stock

Juice of 2 lemons

1 lb (454 g) baby carrots

1 lb (454 g) green beans, trimmed

2 tbsp (16 g) cornstarch

2 tbsp (30 ml) water

2 tbsp (8 g) chopped fresh Italian parsley

Place the potatoes in the bottom of a slow cooker on high heat. I like to use my 6-quart (5.4-L) oval slow cooker. Set aside. Season both sides of the chicken with the seasoning blend, salt and pepper.

Warm a 10-inch (25-cm) skillet over medium-high heat. Once you can feel the heat when you hold your hand 6 inches (15 cm) above the skillet, add 2 tablespoons (30 ml) of the oil. Add the chicken to the skillet in two batches and brown on both sides, about 3 minutes on each side. Add the remaining 2 tablespoons (30 ml) of oil for the next batch and brown the chicken on both sides.

Remove the browned chicken from the skillet and layer it on top of the potatoes in the slow cooker. Add the garlic to the skillet and cook for 30 seconds. Next, add the wine to the skillet and scrape the browned bits from the bottom of the pan while it bubbles. Bring the mixture to a boil for 3 minutes. Add the chicken stock and lemon juice and stir to combine.

Add the carrots to the slow cooker and pour the liquid from the skillet on top. Cover and cook for 2 to 3 hours on high (or 4 to 6 hours on low). Add the green beans to the slow cooker during the last 15 minutes of cooking time.

To thicken the sauce, combine the cornstarch and water in a mason jar. Seal the jar and shake the living tar out of it to create a slurry. Then pour the slurry into the slow cooker for the last 30 minutes of cooking. Sprinkle with the parsley before serving.

DONNA'S SIMPLE KITCHEN TIPS: If you are pressed for time, you can toss all of the ingredients into the slow cooker (reserving the green beans for the last 15 minutes of cooking time and completely excluding the olive oil) and cook for 3 to 4 hours on high. Then place the chicken on a baking sheet and broil in the oven for 3 to 4 minutes until it is browned and crisp.

If you are sensitive to alcohol, you can substitute the wine with more chicken stock.

MEXICAN ROAST BEEF DIP SANDWICH

These sandwiches are a scrumptious Southwestern twist on the original. Living in Arizona, we see and taste a great influence from the southern border, so we were excited to switch things up from the classic French dip sandwich and kick up the flavors! Roast beef is seasoned with Mexican spices and seared to create an unforgettable crust. Then it is slow cooked until it's fall-apart tender. After it's shredded, it is loaded up on a toasty roll, layered with Monterey Jack and cheddar cheeses and then topped with roasted red peppers and banana pepper rings. As if that weren't enough, it's served with a chipotle beef au jus that is absolutely ahhhhhmazing!

3 tbsp (21 g) Mexican Seasoning Blend (page 160)

1 tbsp (18 g) kosher salt

3 lb (1.4 kg) boneless beef chuck roast

2 tbsp (30 ml) extra virgin olive oil

1 (12-oz [355-ml]) bottle Mexican beer

1 cup (235 ml) beef stock

¼ cup (60 ml) freshly squeezed lime juice

6 cloves garlic, minced

4 chipotle chiles in adobo sauce, minced

1 tbsp (15 ml) adobo sauce (from the chipotle chile can)

6 crusty hoagie rolls

6 thick slices Monterey Jack cheese

6 thick slices medium cheddar cheese

Roasted red peppers, for topping

Mild banana pepper rings, for topping

Chopped fresh cilantro, for topping

Combine the Mexican seasoning and salt in a 1-gallon (3.6-L) zip-top bag. Pat the roast dry with paper towels and add the roast to the bag. Seal the bag and shake it until the roast is completely coated. Set aside.

Warm a Dutch oven or heavy-bottomed pot over medium-high heat. Once you can feel the heat when you hold your hand 6 inches (15 cm) above the pot, add the oil. Sear all sides of the roast, 2 to 3 minutes per side. When the roast is nicely seared with a good crust, place it in your slow cooker. Don't skip this step, because it adds layers of flavor that you can't get otherwise.

Return the Dutch oven to the heat and deglaze the pot with the beer. As it bubbles, use a spatula to scrape up the yummy browned bits. Add the beef stock, lime juice, garlic, chipotle peppers and adobo sauce and stir. Bring the liquid to a boil for 3 minutes. Pour the liquid into the slow cooker and cover. Cook for 3 to 4 hours on high (or 6 to 8 hours on low), until the meat is very tender and pulls apart easily. Shred the meat with two forks and allow the shredded beef to cook in the liquid for 30 minutes longer.

Meanwhile, split the rolls and place them on a baking sheet cut side up. Toast in a 425°F (220°C, or gas mark 7) oven until the edges are golden brown, 4 to 5 minutes.

Pile the shredded roast beef on the toasted rolls. Top each roll with 1 slice each of Monterey Jack and cheddar cheese. Place the sandwiches on the baking sheet and warm them in the oven until the cheese is melted, about 4 minutes. Top with roasted red peppers and banana pepper rings. Sprinkle with cilantro. Spoon off the fat from the broth and then pour it through a strainer into a bowl and *voilà*—au jus.

DONNA'S SIMPLE KITCHEN TIPS: When making dip-style sandwiches, you want to use a crusty bread that will hold up to dipping in the juices. French baguette hoagie rolls are the best.

If you are sensitive to alcohol, you can substitute the beer with 1½ cups (355 ml) of additional beef stock.

ITALIAN BASIL-PESTO CHICKEN

This tender, slow-cooked chicken in a fresh basil-pesto sauce takes only 5 minutes of prep. It is a light and scrumptious dinner that is perfect with rice and veggies. The pesto adds an unbelievably fresh and nutty flavor, creating a memorable chicken dinner. Easy chicken dishes are a staple in our kitchen, and it doesn't get simpler than this. Of course, if you don't have time to make the pesto, you can use store-bought. I use the leftovers on my salad during the week and the shredded chicken makes a delicious chicken salad sandwich.

3 lb (1.4 kg) boneless skinless chicken breasts

1 cup (240 g) Perfect Basil Pesto (page 156), divided

½ cup (120 ml) chicken stock

1 tsp crushed red pepper flakes

½ cup (75 g) cherry tomatoes, halved

¼ cup (25 g) freshly shredded Parmesan cheese

Place the chicken breasts in the bottom of your slow cooker. Add ¾ cup (180 g) of the pesto, the chicken stock and the crushed red pepper flakes. Stir to combine and cover. Cook for 2 to 3 hours on high (or 4 to 5 hours on low).

Remove the chicken and place it in a serving dish. Stir the sauce and pour it over the chicken. Spoon the remaining ¼ cup (60 g) of pesto over the chicken breasts. Sprinkle the tomatoes and Parmesan cheese over the chicken. Cover for 10 to 15 minutes to allow the cheese to melt.

DONNA'S SIMPLE KITCHEN TIP: You can also shred the chicken once it's tender enough to pull apart with two forks and let it cook for 30 minutes longer to absorb the liquid.

CHIPOTLE-LIME BARBECUE PORK CHOPS

This is the easiest pork chop recipe ever, because who has the time for cooking long, complicated meals? This is the ultimate toss-and-go meal, because it literally takes 5 minutes to prep. Just add the ingredients to the slow cooker and you return to perfectly tender, melt-in-your-mouth pork cooked in the most spectacular bright and smoky chipotle-lime sauce. I fell in love with a chipotle-lime salad dressing at a restaurant that we love and knew those flavors were destined to become something amazing. I was right. This is a little sweet, a little spicy, a little barbecue-y (yes I made that word up) and a lot delicious. It's so easy that it just about cooks itself . . . well actually, I guess it does. Way to go slow cooker!

½ cup (120 g) ketchup

½ cup (112 g) packed light brown sugar

¼ cup (60 ml) reduced-sodium soy sauce

¼ cup (60 ml) lime juice

2 chipotle chiles in adobo sauce, minced

1 tbsp (15 ml) adobo sauce (from the chipotle chile can)

1 tbsp (6 g) Mexican Seasoning Blend (page 160)

1 tsp kosher salt

3 lb (1.4 kg) thick-cut boneless pork chops (1"–1½" [2.5–3.8 cm])

¼ cup (32 g) cornstarch

¼ cup (60 ml) water

1 tbsp (6 g) lime zest

2 tbsp (8 g) chopped fresh Italian parsley

Combine the ketchup, brown sugar, soy sauce, lime juice, chipotles, adobo, spice blend and salt in a 6-quart (5.4-L) slow cooker. Stir to combine.

Trim the excess fat from the pork chops, if necessary. A thin layer of fat will add to the sauce, but too much is not tasty. Add the pork chops to the slow cooker in an even layer. Spoon a thick layer of sauce over the pork chops. Cover and cook for 4 hours on high.

After 3 hours of cooking, taste the sauce. Season with salt if necessary. Combine the cornstarch and water in a mason jar. Seal the jar and shake the living tar out of it to create a slurry. Add the slurry to the slow cooker. Stir, cover and cook for 1 more hour.

Garnish with the lime zest and parley.

DONNA'S SIMPLE KITCHEN TIP: Chipotles in adobo sauce are found in the international foods aisle in your grocery store near the Mexican sauces. Add chipotles according to your desired heat level. Do not add the whole can. We used two chipotles because we like a little kick. If you prefer it milder, add just one, or omit it altogether. It is fabulous either way.

TWO

ONE-POT WONDERS

I prefer to have very little cleanup to do when I am finished cooking. I really want to get back to my family, not spend the evening in the kitchen washing pots. That is one of the reasons I fell in love with one-pot recipes years ago. But in the last few years, I have discovered the one-pot wonder. The one-pot wonder is the only type of recipe that truly rivals my beloved slow cooker. All one-pots are wonderful—don't get me wrong—but a one-pot wonder is a recipe wherein you can literally dump everything into one pot and let it cook. That's it!

We have several one-pot wonders on our website, The Slow Roasted Italian, and they are crazy popular. Last year, Chad and I were asked to present at a conference. We did a class on one-pot wonders, naturally. People are genuinely amazed that you can drop it all in one pot and cook it. Our favorite part is that the pasta or rice absorbs the delicious liquid in the pot and adds starchiness to it, which creates a rich and thick sauce for your dish that requires very little work.

Our Cheesy Greek Pasta with Chicken (page 33) is my absolute favorite. It is happy dance–worthy and I thought I would try my luck with some friends of ours that own a Greek restaurant. Needless to say, they texted us and asked if they could have the recipe to put on the menu in their restaurant. That's two thumbs up for sure!

The Cheesy Cajun Pasta (page 49) with tender bites of chicken and hot sausage comes in second, and trust me it was a photo finish. This Cajun pasta is cooked in a glorious white wine Alfredo sauce that will rock your world. It did mine!

Mexican Chicken and Rice Casserole (page 38) is one of our family's favorite recipes in the book. I make it nearly every week, portion it out with a scooper and flash freeze it for easy-to-grab meals. There are two options, using chicken (which is a one-pot wonder) or using ground beef, which is our go-to as a family. Either way, everyone devours it, including my picky crew.

Lemon Rosemary Chicken and Rice (page 45) is a glorious one-pot creation that I could eat every day. It is bright and fresh, with perfectly tender and flavorful bites of chicken and crisp-tender asparagus.

Meatball Parmesan Skillet (page 46), Creamy Beef Stroganoff with Egg Noodles (page 50) and Home-Style Chicken and Biscuits (page 42) are the best comfort foods you could ask for. They are traditional one-pot recipes that come together in just 30 minutes. How awesome is that? Actually, every recipe in this chapter is ready in 30 minutes or less, all in one pot! Can you imagine all that flavor in such little time with very little work? Grab your pot and let's get cooking!

CHEESY GREEK PASTA WITH CHICKEN

Our favorite Mediterranean ingredients infuse big, bold flavors in this ambrosial Greek pasta dish. Succulent sun-dried tomatoes, briny kalamata olives, herbed chicken and tender baby spinach all come together in a rich and creamy feta wine sauce. It's most definitely my favorite one-pot wonder and it's ready in just 30 minutes. Let's just say it's so good I broke out into my happy dance! My family knows that if they see me dancing with my food in the kitchen . . . dinner's going to be incredible!

1 cup (110 g) sun-dried tomatoes packed in oil and Italian herbs, drained

1 large yellow onion, sliced

1 lb (454 g) boneless, skinless chicken breasts, cut into ½" (1.3-cm) pieces

6 cloves garlic, sliced

1 cup (100 g) kalamata olives, pitted and halved

1 lb (454 g) linguine pasta, uncooked

2 tsp (2 g) dried oregano

1 tsp freshly ground pepper

1 tsp kosher salt

8 cups (240 g) baby spinach leaves, divided

4 cups (940 ml) chicken stock

1 cup (235 ml) Chardonnay

8 oz (227 g) feta cheese, crumbled

Combine the tomatoes, onion, chicken, garlic, olives, linguine, oregano, pepper and salt with 4 cups (120 g) of the spinach in a 12-inch (30.5-cm) braising pan or Dutch oven over medium-high heat. Pour the chicken stock and the wine over the top.

Cover and bring to a boil. Cook for 7 to 9 minutes, until the pasta is al dente (has a bite to it). Toss the pasta with tongs occasionally to keep it from sticking to the bottom of the pot. You will still have some liquid in the pan when the pasta is done cooking; this is going to make the base for our delicious cheese sauce.

Turn off the heat and add the cheese to the pasta. Toss the pasta with tongs until the cheese melts into the pasta. Toss in the remaining 4 cups (120 g) of spinach.

DONNA'S SIMPLE KITCHEN TIP: Grab two lids of the same size. You can use plasticware or lids from your fridge. Place one lid with the lip facing up, so you have an edge that will hold your food. Fill the lid with kalamata olives. Place the second lid on top of the olives with the lip facing down. Firmly press down on the top lid. The two lips will hold the olives in place, so they do not roll off the lid. Slide your serrated knife between the lids and carefully slice through them. Watch your fingers. Now you have halved olives in the blink of an eye!

CHICKEN BROCCOLI ALFREDO WITH FETTUCCINI

This is a glorious dish that starts with tender pan-fried chicken breast finished in a luxurious Chardonnay cream sauce that will blow your mind. Chicken and broccoli are an amazing combination, and I just can't get enough.

2 tbsp (28 g) unsalted butter

1 lb (454 g) boneless skinless chicken breast, cut into bite-size pieces

½ tsp kosher salt

½ tsp ground black pepper

1 cup (235 ml) Chardonnay

1 cup (235 ml) reduced-sodium chicken stock

1 cup (235 ml) half-and-half

8 oz (228 g) uncooked fettuccini (or whatever pasta you prefer)

2 cups (140 g) broccoli florets

2 cups (200 g) freshly grated Parmesan cheese

¼ tsp freshly ground nutmeg

Chopped fresh Italian parsley, for garnish (optional)

Warm a 10-inch (25.4-cm) skillet over medium-high heat and add the butter. Once the butter is melted, add the chicken and sprinkle it with the salt and pepper. Cook until the chicken is browned, about 5 minutes. Add the wine to the skillet, and scrape the browned bits from the bottom of the skillet. Bring the wine to a boil. Add the stock and half-and-half. Stir to combine the sauce.

Add the uncooked fettuccini to the skillet. Stir to combine and coat the pasta in the sauce (the pasta will cook right in the sauce, absorbing it and becoming incredibly flavorful). Bring the sauce to a boil. Once it's boiling, cover the pan and cook for 5 minutes. Add the broccoli and cook 4 to 5 minutes longer, until the pasta is al dente (has a bite to it). Remove from the heat. Stir in the Parmesan cheese and nutmeg. If necessary, add salt and pepper to taste. Garnish with the fresh parsley, if desired.

The sauce will thicken as it cools. If the sauce gets too thick, you can add a splash of chicken stock and give it a stir to loosen it up.

DONNA'S SIMPLE KITCHEN TIP: If you are sensitive to alcohol, you can substitute the Chardonnay for white grape juice or chicken stock. Look for the chicken stock in the yellow box with reduced sodium but full flavor!

FARMERS' MARKET PASTA WITH SAUSAGE

I absolutely love veggies and rarely do I have an occasion to make a veggie lover's dinner. Truth be told, this is absolutely perfect for a night with the girls or for my lunches all week long. I love strolling through the store and the markets all year round, but especially during the summer, and loading up with my favorite veggies, then coming home and creating light and fresh meals. I actually went a little lighter on the pasta (shocking, I know) and I also used chicken sausage, but you can use your favorite. The rich and juicy tomatoes cook into this absolutely glorious sauce that will blow your mind. It's fresh and decadent all at the same time. Not to mention, you get to enjoy a dinner that feels lighter, so it makes you feel much better about indulging in those No-Bake Rocky Road Avalanche Bars (page 166). It's all about balance, my friends. You're welcome!

3 cups (450 g) assorted grape tomatoes, sliced in half lengthwise, divided

8 oz (227 g) penne pasta, uncooked

1 lb (454 g) smoked sausage, sliced into coins

1 small red onion, sliced

1 red bell pepper, cored, seeded and cut into bite-size pieces

1 yellow bell pepper, cored, seeded and cut into bite-size pieces

4 cloves garlic, sliced

1 tsp kosher salt

1 tsp freshly ground black pepper

2½ cups (590 ml) water

1 broccoli crown, florets cut into bite-size pieces (about 2 cups [140 g])

1 lb (454 g) asparagus, trimmed and cut into bite-size pieces (about 2 cups [300 g])

Combine 2 cups (300 g) of the tomatoes, pasta, sausage, onion, bell peppers, garlic, salt, pepper and water in a 3-quart (2.7-L) braising pan or large pot over medium-high heat. Cover and bring to a boil. Once the water is boiling, remove the lid and cook for 9 to 11 minutes, until the pasta is al dente (has a bite to it). Five minutes before the pasta is done, stir in the broccoli and asparagus. When it is done the liquid will be transformed into a luxurious fresh tomato sauce. Add the remaining 1 cup (150 g) of tomatoes and stir to combine.

DONNA'S SIMPLE KITCHEN TIP: To quickly clean and cut a bell pepper, cut off the top and bottom of the pepper, then slice it down the side and unfold it into a flat sheet. Run your chef's knife along the inside of the pepper to remove the membrane and seeds. Once it is cleaned, you can slice it evenly and chop it into bite-size pieces. My mom taught me not to waste, so I go back and cut the stem out of the lid and chop up the top and bottom into bite-size pieces.

MEXICAN CHICKEN AND RICE CASSEROLE

Our family is wild about Mexican flavors, and this casserole is on the menu every week. Sierra eats it almost every day for lunch. It is the perfect one-pot wonder that our entire family asks for, and it's made with ingredients that we always have on hand. Just dump it in the pot and go. It doesn't get much easier than that! Tender chicken comes together with tomatoes, black beans, corn, jalapeños and rice to create this simple recipe that will knock your socks off. It's smoky, spicy and so hearty. We love this with tortilla chips, but it's perfect just on a spoon!

1½ lb (680 g) chicken breast, cut into ½"–¾" (1.3–1.9-cm) pieces

2 cups (470 ml) reduced-sodium chicken stock

1 cup (190 g) uncooked jasmine rice

1 (15-oz [425-ml]) can reduced-sodium black beans, rinsed and drained

1 (14.5-oz [410-ml]) can fire-roasted tomatoes with garlic

1 cup (130 g) frozen corn

1 (4-oz [112-g]) can fire-roasted diced green chiles

2 tbsp (14 g) Mexican Seasoning Blend (page 160)

1 tsp kosher salt

2 cups (240 g) freshly shredded Colby Jack cheese

Chopped fresh cilantro, for garnish (optional)

Warm a 10-inch (25.4-cm) oven-safe skillet over medium-high heat. Add the chicken, chicken stock, rice, black beans, tomatoes, corn, chiles, seasoning blend and salt. Stir to combine. Cover and bring to a boil. Stir well, making sure there are no bits stuck to the bottom. Cover and reduce the heat to a simmer. Cook for 15 minutes, or until the rice is cooked through. Stir halfway through the cooking time to make sure no bits are stuck to the bottom of the pan. Taste for seasoning, and add salt as necessary.

Remove the skillet from the heat and sprinkle with the cheese. Place the skillet under the broiler until the cheese is completely melted, about 2 minutes. Or you can skip the broiler and stir it in until it's completely melted. Sprinkle with cilantro, if desired.

DONNA'S SIMPLE KITCHEN TIP: If you prefer ground beef, you can fry the ground beef with the salt until cooked through. Then sprinkle the spices over the top and mix until well-coated. Add the remaining ingredients (using water instead of chicken stock) and finish the recipe as written. I make it weekly and flash freeze scoops of it for quick lunches. Reheat with a splash of water and you have an easy meal anytime.

TEX-MEX PASTA AND SAUSAGE

This dish features a spectacular Texas-style Mexican-inspired sauce that is cooked right into the fettuccini. We fell in love with Tex-Mex flavors long ago, but a recent visit to Houston—and a food tour of the delicious town while we were visiting Chad's dad—really brought it home. The hot smoked sausage provides all the seasoning you will need; combined with our favorite Tex-Mex veggies and pasta, it creates a fresh and smoky knock-your-boots-off meal that is so easy it just about cooks itself. Now that's my kind of meal!

3 cups (450 g) halved grape tomatoes, divided

2 tbsp (2 g) chopped fresh cilantro, divided

1 lb (454 g) hot smoked sausage, sliced into coins

1 lb (454 g) fettuccini, uncooked

1 cup (130 g) sweet corn kernels (fresh, canned or frozen)

1 cup (250 g) canned black beans, rinsed and drained

1 small white onion, sliced

1 orange bell pepper, cored, seeded and chopped

1 jalapeño pepper, sliced into coins

4 cloves garlic, sliced

1½ tsp kosher salt

1 tsp fresh ground pepper

5 cups (1.2 L) water

Combine 2 cups (300 g) of the tomatoes, 1 tablespoon (1 g) of the cilantro, the sausage, fettuccini, corn, beans, onion, bell pepper, jalapeño, garlic, salt, pepper and water in a Dutch oven or large 6-quart (5.4-L) pot over medium-high heat. Cover and bring to a boil. Once the water is boiling, remove the lid and cook for 7 to 9 minutes, until the pasta is al dente (has a bite to it). Toss the pasta with tongs occasionally to keep it from sticking. The liquid will be mostly absorbed when the pasta is finished cooking.

Add the remaining 1 cup (150 g) of tomatoes and the remaining 1 tablespoon (1 g) of cilantro and toss to combine.

DONNA'S SIMPLE KITCHEN TIP: If you love Tex-Mex but don't prefer the heat, you can swap half of a 7-ounce (196-g) can of fire-roasted green chiles for the jalapeño and use regular smoked sausage. Or if you prefer, you can make it as is and serve it with a dollop of sour cream. The cream will cool down the dish and still offer the same delicious flavor.

HOME-STYLE CHICKEN AND BISCUITS

Chicken and biscuits ranks high on our comfort food radar! Not surprisingly, chicken and biscuits is a specialty in the Midwest and in the South. I mean, what could be better than tender chunks of chicken cooked in a rich and flavorful cream sauce with carrots and peas? How about light and fluffy Parmesan cheese drop biscuits, to really take this dish over the top? Dinner's ready!

CHICKEN

4 tbsp (56 g) unsalted butter

1 cup (120 g) diced carrots

1 small shallot, diced

¼ cup (30 g) all-purpose flour

1 tbsp (3 g) Tuscan-Style Seasoning Blend (page 160)

2 tsp (12 g) kosher salt

½ tsp black pepper

3 cups (705 ml) reduced-sodium chicken stock

2 lb (908 g) boneless skinless chicken breasts, cut into ½" (1.3-cm) pieces

1 cup (235 ml) whole milk

1 cup (130 g) frozen peas

BISCUITS

4 tbsp (56 g) unsalted butter, divided

2 cups (240 g) all-purpose flour

1 tbsp (12 g) baking powder

1 tbsp (12 g) sugar

1 tbsp (8 g) garlic powder

¾ tsp kosher salt, divided

1 cup (235 ml) whole milk

2 cups (200 g) freshly shredded Parmesan cheese

½ tsp dried parsley

Preheat the oven to 450°F (230°C, or gas mark 8).

To make the chicken, melt the butter in a 4-quart (3.6-L) braising pan or 12-inch (30.5-cm) oven-safe skillet over medium-high heat. Add the carrots and shallot. Cook until the shallot is softened, 2 to 3 minutes, stirring occasionally. Sprinkle the flour, seasoning blend, salt and pepper over the vegetables and stir to coat completely. Cook for 1 minute to cook out the floury taste.

Add the chicken stock, chicken pieces, milk and peas to the pan. Bring to a boil and then reduce the heat to a simmer. Cover the pot and cook for 5 minutes.

Meanwhile, to make the biscuits, add 2 tablespoons (28 g) of the butter to a large microwave-safe mixing bowl. Microwave for 30 seconds, or until the butter is melted. Add the flour, baking powder, sugar, garlic powder and ½ teaspoon of the salt. Stir until combined. Pour in the milk and stir just until the flour is all wet; do not overmix. Fold in the cheese.

Uncover the pot and drop heaping spoonfuls of biscuits on top of the chicken stew. Transfer to the oven and bake for 10 to 12 minutes, until golden brown.

Melt the remaining 2 tablespoons (28 g) of butter in a small bowl. Add the remaining ¼ teaspoon of salt and the parsley. Stir with a pastry brush. Remove the pan from the oven and brush the biscuits with the melted butter mixture.

DONNA'S SIMPLE KITCHEN TIP: Shallots have a mild and slightly sweet onion flavor with a hint of garlic. They have less bite than an onion and are perfect in dishes where they will be eaten raw or if you are looking for a mild onion flavor. You can substitute 3 small shallots per 1 small onion in recipes.

LEMON ROSEMARY CHICKEN AND RICE

One of our favorite things about where we live is our prolific lemon tree. Our second favorite is all of the rosemary bushes we planted in my backyard. Chad and I could live on lemon rosemary combinations, and this one-pot chicken meal is no exception. Juicy chicken, nutty jasmine rice and crisp-tender asparagus are cooked in a rosemary lemon sauce that will blow your mind. Look out, happy dance!

2 tbsp (30 ml) extra virgin olive oil

1½ lb (680 g) boneless skinless chicken breasts, cut into bite-size cubes

1 tsp kosher salt

½ tsp freshly ground black pepper

1 cup (190 g) jasmine rice

1 tbsp (2 g) chopped fresh rosemary

1 tsp garlic powder

1 tsp onion powder

2 cups (470 ml) chicken stock

Zest and juice of 1 lemon

1 bunch asparagus, trimmed and cut into 1″ (2.5-cm) pieces

In a 10-inch (25.4-cm) skillet over medium heat, warm the olive oil. Once you can feel the heat when you hold your hand 6 inches (15 cm) above the skillet, add the chicken and sprinkle with the salt and pepper. Cook until the chicken is browned on the outside, stirring occasionally, 7 to 10 minutes. We are going to cook it some more, so it's okay if it is not cooked through yet.

Add the rice, rosemary, garlic powder, onion powder, chicken stock and lemon juice. Stir to combine, cover and bring everything to a boil. Once it is boiling, reduce the heat to a simmer. Cook for 8 minutes, and then stir and add the asparagus.

Cook until the asparagus is crisp-tender, 5 to 7 minutes longer. Sprinkle with the lemon zest.

DONNA'S SIMPLE KITCHEN TIP: To trim asparagus, bend the spear. It will snap into two pieces, dividing the tender asparagus from the woody root end.

MEATBALL PARMESAN SKILLET

I just can't get enough meatballs. I try them everywhere we go; there really should be a permanent place for meatballs on every menu. I love using meatballs in creative ways, such as in soups, on pizza, in salads and in this one-skillet recipe, a fun twist on the classic chicken Parmesan. In this recipe, tender Italian herb meatballs are cooked in a spicy Arrabbiata marinara and topped with two kinds of cheese. Oh my heavens! Somebody hold me, I may need a moment here.

2 tbsp (30 ml) extra virgin olive oil

1 recipe Italian Herb Baked Meatballs, uncooked (page 143)

1 recipe 10-Minute Marinara Arrabbiata (page 147)

2 cups (240 g) freshly shredded mozzarella cheese

1 cup (100 g) freshly shredded Parmesan cheese

2 tbsp (5 g) chopped fresh basil

2 tbsp (8 g) chopped fresh Italian parsley

Preheat the oven to 375°F (190°C, or gas mark 5).

Place a 12-inch (30-cm) cast-iron (or oven-safe) skillet over medium heat. Add the olive oil to the skillet. Using a 2-tablespoon (30-g) scoop, portion out a meatball and roll it into a ball. Place the meatball into the skillet. Continue scooping, rolling and placing the meatballs in the skillet.

Keep an eye on the meatballs and flip them over once they are golden brown. After all the meatballs have been turned at least once, pour the marinara sauce over the meatballs. Place the skillet in the preheated oven. Bake for 15 minutes, or until the meatballs are cooked through.

Sprinkle the meatballs with the mozzarella and Parmesan cheeses and continue baking until the cheese is melted, 3 to 5 minutes. Remove from the oven and sprinkle with the basil and parsley.

DONNA'S SIMPLE KITCHEN TIP: Place soft cheese, like mozzarella, in the freezer for 10 to 15 minutes before shredding to get a cleaner grating. You can also spray your cheese grater with nonstick cooking spray to keep the cheese from sticking.

CHEESY CAJUN PASTA

Tender bites of chicken, spicy sausage, fresh veggies, pasta and an amazing Cajun white wine Alfredo sauce come together to create a recipe that will make you want to lick your plate clean. This recipe is so easy: You just toss the ingredients in the pot and go. It doesn't get much simpler than that. Cajun flavors are rich, bold, a little spicy and a whole lot memorable. Those flavors take me back to an amazing trip that Chad, Sierra and I took to New Orleans a few years ago. It has to be one of the most delicious cities that we have eaten our way through. Thank goodness for all the walking we did or we may have had to roll ourselves home.

1 lb (454 g) boneless skinless chicken breasts, cubed

14 oz (392 g) hot smoked sausage, sliced

2 bell peppers, cored, seeded and sliced (I use red and green)

1 medium yellow onion, sliced

1 lb (454 g) campanelle pasta (trumpet-shaped), uncooked

4 cups (940 ml) chicken stock

1 cup (235 ml) Chardonnay

2 tbsp (12 g) Cajun spice mix (see Tip)

1 tsp kosher salt

2 cups (200 g) freshly shredded Parmesan cheese

½ cup (120 ml) heavy cream

2 tbsp (8 g) chopped fresh Italian parsley

Combine the chicken, sausage, peppers, onion, pasta, chicken stock, wine, spice mix and salt in a Dutch oven or 12-inch (30-cm) braising pan. Stir to combine. Cover and bring to a boil. Remove the cover and cook until the pasta is al dente (has a bite to it), 10 to 12 minutes, stirring occasionally to keep the pasta from sticking.

Remove from the heat and add the Parmesan cheese. Stir until the cheese melts into the pasta. Add the cream and stir to combine. Sprinkle with the parsley.

DONNA'S SIMPLE KITCHEN TIP: You can make your own homemade Cajun spice mix by combining 1 teaspoon cayenne pepper, 1 teaspoon paprika, 1 teaspoon garlic powder, 1 teaspoon onion powder, 1 teaspoon dried oregano, ½ teaspoon kosher salt and ½ teaspoon black pepper.

CREAMY BEEF STROGANOFF WITH EGG NOODLES

Beef stroganoff is pure comfort food that all starts with scrumptious seared sirloin steak and tons of fresh mushrooms in a rich and creamy brown gravy with egg noodles that comes together very simply in one pot! I honestly was vocally opposed to mushrooms for many years. Very vocally . . . that is, until I found fresh mushrooms. They are so much different in flavor and texture compared to the jarred variety I had growing up. This recipe is truly a revelation and a celebration of my ever-evolving palate and proof that if you don't like something, you probably haven't had it cooked the right way for you yet.

1 lb (454 g) sirloin steak, cut into bite-size pieces

2 tsp (12 g) kosher salt, divided, more to taste

2 tsp (4 g) freshly ground black pepper, divided, more to taste

4 tbsp (60 ml) extra virgin olive oil, divided

8 oz (227 g) sliced cremini mushrooms

8 oz (227 g) sliced white button mushrooms

½ medium yellow onion, sliced

4 cloves garlic, minced

1 cup (235 ml) Chardonnay

8 oz (227 g) wide egg noodles, uncooked

4 cups (940 ml) beef stock, divided

2 tbsp (30 ml) Worcestershire sauce

2 tbsp (16 g) cornstarch

½ cup (120 g) sour cream

2 tsp (30 g) Dijon mustard

2 tbsp (8 g) chopped fresh Italian parsley

Season the steak pieces with 1 teaspoon of the salt and 1 teaspoon of the pepper. Warm a 3-quart (2.7-L) braising pan or Dutch oven over medium-high heat. Once you can feel the heat when you hold your hand 6 inches (15 cm) above the pan, add 2 tablespoons (30 ml) of the oil. Swirl the oil around the pan and immediately add the steak pieces in a single layer. The pan will sizzle and hiss when you add the steak. If it doesn't make a big fuss, it isn't ready yet.

Allow the steak to sear for 2 to 3 minutes before touching it. Flip the steak pieces over and allow the steak to sear on the second side for 2 to 3 minutes. Remove the steak pieces from the pan and place them on a plate.

Add the remaining 2 tablespoons (30 ml) of olive oil to the skillet and add the cremini and white button mushrooms, onion and garlic. Cook the vegetables until they are browned, about 5 minutes, stirring occasionally.

Pour the Chardonnay into the pan and scrape the browned bits off the bottom of the pan. Add the egg noodles, 3¾ cups (880 ml) of the beef stock and the Worcestershire sauce. Stir to combine. Cover the pan and bring to a boil. Remove the cover and stir occasionally until the egg noodles are cooked al dente (has a bite to it), 6 to 8 minutes.

Meanwhile, create a slurry by combining the cornstarch and remaining ¼ cup (60 ml) of beef stock in a mason jar. Seal and shake the living tar out of it, until there are no lumps. Pour in the slurry and stir occasionally until the sauce is thickened, 1 to 2 minutes. Remove the pan from the heat and add the sour cream and Dijon. Stir until combined. Add the steak back to the pan and stir to combine. Taste for seasoning. Add the remaining 1 teaspoon salt and remaining 1 teaspoon pepper to taste. Sprinkle with the parsley.

DONNA'S SIMPLE KITCHEN TIP: Cremini mushrooms are also known as baby bella, because they are baby portobello mushrooms. They have a deeper, heartier and more complex, earthy flavor than their immature cousin 'shroom, the white button. White buttons are softer and have a subtler woodsy flavor with a hint of earthiness. You can pick these both up at the grocery store pre-sliced to save yourself some prep time.

THREE

DINNER IN A SNAP!

Time is a huge commodity in our lives (I am sure you can relate). Between our business, school activities for our daughter, sports and playdates, hanging out with friends, taking family time and then trying to save enough time for a date night for me and Chad, it's a lot to put together. So, like most people, I value every last minute of my day.

I have been making 30-minute recipes for many years, but sometimes 30 minutes is just too long. Can I get an "Amen!"? Eating out is such an easy option, but more often than not, a quick dinner amounts to a disappointing fast food experience. So, I started creating quick and easy dinners that I am excited to feed my family and that are absolutely bursting with flavor. I mean, if I am going to take the time to cook dinner, the payoff needs to be worth it, and these "dinner in a snap" recipes do not disappoint!

This chapter is packed with quick and easy recipes with a huge flavor reward! Most of these recipes are ready in 20 minutes and there are a few others to shake things up.

Chili Lime Steak Bites (page 55) are always a big hit! Perfectly seared, tender steak in a spicy chili and tart lime sauce create an absolutely crave-worthy dish in just 15 minutes. Everyone goes crazy over them, and Chad and I can't keep our hands off them. I have made them at least a dozen times and every last time the family was in the kitchen swarming the pan. Know what I mean?

Tuscan Garlic Chicken and Linguine (page 56) is a rich, luscious, special occasion–worthy meal that the whole family will love. I dream about that Chardonnay cream sauce! It's a taste of your favorite Italian restaurant, at home in 20 minutes.

The entire family has enjoyed the Cheesy Taco Skillet (page 59) over and over. It comes together in 15 minutes in one pan and is perfect for a low-key dinner. Leftovers make a wonderful salad topping!

You know we love our comfort food, and the Creamy Bacon Carbonara with Peas (page 63) is just that. It is a rich and creamy meal that is utterly amazing.

Sierra was completely over the moon with the Cheesy Jalapeño Popper Quesadillas (page 67), and I have to say we all love them. They are a fun game-day twist on the traditional quesadilla and not one bite goes to waste. It is a quick and easy dinner and perfect for lunch, too.

When you can have a delicious dinner ready quicker than you can get takeout, dinner at home becomes, well, a snap! Ready, set, cook.

CHILI LIME STEAK BITES

These steak bites are seared to perfection with a punch of spicy chiles and tart lime to wake up your senses. They are tender and flavorful with an extraordinary Mexican combination that is enough to make your mouth do the tango. Oh, who am I kidding? It's good enough to make me do the happy dance! Chad and I completely and uncontrollably devour 'em. They are darned near addictive. I usually make two batches because of my utter lack of self-control when it comes to these steak bites.

1 lb (454 g) top sirloin steak

½ tsp kosher salt

½ tsp black pepper

½ tsp garlic powder

2 tbsp (30 g) chili paste

1 tbsp (20 g) honey

2 tbsp (30 ml) extra virgin olive oil

2 limes, zested and juiced

Cut the steak into 1-inch (2.5-cm) strips. Then cut again into ½-inch (1.3-cm) pieces. Place the steak in a small bowl and sprinkle with the salt, pepper and garlic powder. Stir until the steak is completely coated. Add the chili paste and honey. Stir again until all the steak bites are coated in the mixture.

Place a 10-inch (25.4-cm) cast-iron skillet over medium-high heat. Once you can feel the heat when you hold your hand 6 inches (15 cm) above the pan, add the oil. Swirl the oil around the pan and immediately add the steak bites in a single layer. The pan will sizzle and hiss when you add the steak. If it doesn't make a big fuss, it isn't ready yet.

Allow the steak to sear for 1 minute before touching it. Flip the steak bites over. You can use tongs, or a spatula works great to flip a whole bunch at once. Allow the steak to sear on the second side for 1 minute. Remove the steak from the pan and place on a plate. Add the lime zest and lime juice to the hot pan. Stir to combine and pour the chili lime sauce over the steak bites.

DONNA'S SIMPLE KITCHEN TIP: Making deliciousness out of a quick recipe is as simple as using the right ingredients. This recipe is the perfect example. Choose a steak that is great for high-heat searing and quick cooking with great flavor. You want a well-marbled cut that is tender enough to stand up to searing, such as a strip, rib eye or top sirloin, to make the best steak bites.

TUSCAN GARLIC CHICKEN AND LINGUINE

Tender and juicy chicken with linguine pasta and fresh red peppers are tossed in a rich and creamy Chardonnay-garlic-cream sauce to create this Tuscan-inspired dish. There is nothing quite like a restaurant-style dinner that comes together in just 20 minutes in your own kitchen. It is kind of like a little taste of Italy at home.

1 tsp kosher salt, plus more for pasta water

1 lb (454 g) linguine pasta, uncooked

3 tbsp (45 ml) extra virgin olive oil

1 lb (454 g) boneless skinless chicken breasts

½ tsp freshly ground black pepper

4 cloves garlic, minced

2 red bell peppers, cored, seeded and cut into thin strips

¼ tsp crushed red pepper flakes

1 cup (235 ml) Chardonnay

2 tsp (2 g) Tuscan-Style Seasoning Blend (page 160)

2 cups (470 ml) half-and-half

1 cup (100 g) freshly shredded Parmesan cheese

5 oz (140 g) fresh spinach

¼ cup (16 g) chopped fresh Italian parsley

Bring a pot of water to a boil over high heat. Add a small handful of salt and the linguine and cook until it's al dente (has a bite to it). Drain the pasta and reserve 2 cups (470 ml) of the pasta water.

Meanwhile, warm a 10-inch (25.4-cm) skillet over medium-high heat. Once you can feel the heat when you hold your hand 6 inches (15 cm) above the skillet, add the oil. Season both sides of the chicken with the salt and pepper. Add the chicken to the skillet. Cook the chicken until it's a deep golden brown and completely cooked through, 3 to 5 minutes on each side. Remove the chicken and place it on a plate.

Add the garlic, bell peppers and red pepper flakes to the skillet and cook until the peppers are crisp-tender, about 3 minutes, stirring occasionally. Add the wine and seasoning blend to the skillet and scrape the browned bits from the bottom of the pan. Bring the wine to a boil for 2 minutes. Add the half-and-half and the Parmesan cheese. Stir until the cheese melts into the sauce, about 1 minute. Add the reserved pasta water, a ladleful at a time, to thin the sauce if necessary. Sprinkle in the spinach and add the pasta.

Twirl the pasta and spinach into the sauce with tongs. Top with the cooked chicken. Sprinkle with the parsley.

DONNA'S SIMPLE KITCHEN TIP: Covering your pot while bringing it to a boil will cut your cooking time. Be sure not to leave it unattended, or you may have a boil-over to clean up.

If you are sensitive to alcohol, you can substitute the Chardonnay for chicken stock.

CHEESY TACO SKILLET

Our entire family loves this taco skillet. It is a hearty and delicious way to enjoy Taco Tuesday, and it's ready in just 15 minutes. Loaded with your favorite taco flavors, seasoned beef, black beans, corn and fire-roasted tomatoes, it is perfect served with tortilla chips any night of the week or for game day. Simply place the skillet in the center of the table and let diners serve themselves. It doesn't get much easier than that.

2 lb (908 g) lean ground beef (about 88% lean)

2 tsp (12 g) kosher salt, divided

¼ cup (28 g) Mexican Seasoning Blend (page 160)

1 (15-oz [425-g]) can reduced-sodium black beans, rinsed and drained

1 (14.5-oz [410-g]) can fire-roasted tomatoes with garlic

1 (15.25-oz [427-g]) can niblet corn, rinsed and drained (or 1 cup [130 g] frozen corn)

½ cup (120 ml) water

2 cups (240 g) freshly shredded Colby Jack cheese

Tortilla strips, for serving (optional)

Chopped scallions, for serving (optional)

Warm a 10-inch (25.4-cm) skillet over medium-high heat. Once you can feel the heat when you hold your hand 6 inches (15 cm) above the pan, add the ground beef and 1 teaspoon of the salt. Cook, stirring, until the beef is cooked through. Drain the excess drippings if necessary (I had very few drippings). Sprinkle the seasoning and remaining 1 teaspoon of salt over the beef. Stir until the beef is completely coated with the seasoning. Add the black beans, tomatoes, corn and water. Stir to combine.

Bring to a boil, until most of the water is evaporated, about 3 minutes. Sprinkle the cheese on top and stir. Sprinkle with the tortilla strips and scallions, if desired.

DONNA'S SIMPLE KITCHEN TIP: Pre-shredded cheeses have additives to help keep the cheese from sticking together, called anti-caking agents. They also change the way the cheese melts and will cause thickening of your recipes. Skip the pre-shredded cheese and grate your own. All of my recipes call for freshly shredded cheese. I store it in a zip-top bag in the fridge and it keeps for several weeks.

GARLIC SHRIMP WITH LEMON BUTTER CREAM SAUCE

You are not going to want to pass this one up. Succulent shrimp is cooked to perfection and combined with a rich and creamy citrus butter sauce worthy of a special occasion. This recipe is great served over nutty jasmine rice or steamed vegetables. Chad could not get enough and anything this good that is ready in 20 minutes is perfect for my kitchen!

8 tbsp (112 g) unsalted butter, divided

4 cloves garlic, minced

½ tsp crushed red pepper flakes

2 lb (908 g) large shrimp, peeled and deveined

1½ tsp (9 g) kosher salt

1 tsp freshly cracked black pepper

½ cup (120 ml) fresh lemon juice

½ cup (120 ml) heavy cream

¼ cup (16 g) chopped fresh Italian parsley, divided

In a large skillet over medium-high heat, melt 2 tablespoons (28 g) of the butter. Add the garlic and red pepper flakes to the skillet and cook for about 1 minute. Add the shrimp, salt and pepper and cook for 1 minute without stirring. Then stir and continue cooking until the shrimp begin turning pink, 2 to 3 minutes. Remove the shrimp from the pan and set aside in a bowl. Don't worry if they aren't completely cooked; they will be returned to the skillet to continue cooking.

Add the lemon juice to the skillet and bring it to a boil. Cook until the liquid is reduced by half, about 3 minutes. Add the remaining 6 tablespoons (84 g) butter and the cream. Cook until the butter is melted, stirring occasionally. Add half of the parsley and add the shrimp back into the pan. Stir to combine everything. Continue cooking until the shrimp are opaque, 2 to 3 minutes, stirring occasionally. Sprinkle with the remaining half of the parsley.

DONNA'S SIMPLE KITCHEN TIP: Prep all of your ingredients before you begin cooking. Do not skip this step. The cooking goes very quickly in this recipe, so save yourself the stress and be prepared.

SERVES 6

CREAMY BACON CARBONARA WITH PEAS

Here, linguine is tossed in a luxuriously rich and creamy Parmesan cheese sauce with crisp smoky bacon and sweet peas. When I first moved out on my own, a bowl of pasta with a pat of butter and a sprinkle of Parm was my go-to comfort food. Well, I grew up and my palate bloomed. So let's say this is my comfort food all grown up.

1 tsp kosher salt, to taste (plus more for pasta water)

1 lb (454 g) linguine pasta, uncooked

4 oz (112 g) thick-cut bacon, cut into bite-size pieces

2 large eggs

1 cup (235 ml) heavy cream

4 cloves garlic, minced

8 oz (227 g) freshly shredded Parmesan cheese, divided

½ cup (65 g) frozen peas

½ tsp fresh ground black pepper

Handful of fresh flat-leaf parsley, chopped

Bring a 4-quart (3.6-L) pot of salted water to a boil over high heat. Once it boils, add a small handful of salt and the pasta. Lower the heat to medium-high and cook, uncovered, until the pasta is al dente (has a bite to it). Reserve 1 cup (235 ml) of the pasta water. Drain and set aside.

Meanwhile, warm a 12-inch (30.5-cm) skillet over medium-high heat. Sprinkle the bacon into the skillet and cook until crisp, stirring occasionally as needed.

While the bacon is cooking, combine the eggs and cream in a medium bowl. Whisk to combine. Set aside.

Once the bacon is cooked, add the garlic to the skillet. Cook for about 30 seconds. Add the pasta to the skillet and use tongs to toss the pasta in the bacon drippings. Remove the pan from the heat. Add the egg mixture to the pasta and toss with the tongs (work quickly to prevent the eggs from scrambling). Add the Parmesan cheese, peas and pepper. Toss to combine. Thin out the sauce with the reserved pasta water, adding a little at a time until it reaches your desired consistency.

Taste for seasoning and add the remaining 1 teaspoon of salt if necessary. Sprinkle with the fresh parsley.

DONNA'S SIMPLE KITCHEN TIP: Kosher salt has a coarse texture, so it is easy to grab and sprinkle right where you want it. To substitute using table salt, start with half the amount of kosher salt called for and increase to taste. You can always add more.

CREAMY PESTO CHICKEN TORTELLINI

This dish is rich and velvety, with a peppery bite from the basil-pesto cheese sauce. With tender chicken and tortellini that cook right in the sauce, this dish was destined to be all mine! It's a simple one-pot meal and it comes together in a snap. It is the perfect amount of creamy pesto sauce and cheesy goodness, and you won't be able to stop eating it. When I first made it, I planned on enjoying it for lunch throughout the week. Well, that was until Chad tried it. Pesto was never his thing, which I was counting on, but he took one bite, and that was it. He grabbed a bowl and declared it amazing. I need a sign that says, "Donna's Kitchen: converting picky eaters one dinner at a time."

2 tbsp (30 ml) extra virgin olive oil

1½ lb (680 g) boneless skinless chicken breast, cut into bite-size pieces

1 tsp kosher salt

2 cups (470 ml) half-and-half

1 cup (252 g) Perfect Basil Pesto (page 156)

½ tsp crushed red pepper flakes

12 oz (340 g) refrigerated cheese-filled tortellini

1 cup (150 g) grape tomatoes, halved

½ tsp freshly cracked black pepper

1 cup (100 g) freshly grated Parmesan cheese

Warm a 10-inch (25.4-cm) skillet over medium-high heat. Once you can feel the heat when you hold your hand 6 inches (15 cm) above the skillet, add the olive oil and swirl the pan. Add the chicken and sprinkle with the salt. Cook the chicken until it's golden brown, 5 to 6 minutes, stirring occasionally. We will be cooking the chicken longer, so it does not need to be cooked through yet.

Add the half-and-half, pesto and red pepper flakes to the skillet. Cover the pan and bring it to a boil. Once the pesto sauce is boiling, add the tortellini and continue cooking for 7 to 9 minutes, or until the tortellini are cooked through.

Add the grape tomatoes and black pepper. Stir to combine. Sprinkle with the Parmesan cheese.

DONNA'S SIMPLE KITCHEN TIP: To quickly halve grape tomatoes (or grapes, for that matter), grab two lids that are the same size. Place them on the counter with the lips of the lids facing each other, so you have an edge that will hold your food. Fill the bottom lid with cherry tomatoes. Firmly press down on the top lid, but do not squish your tomatoes. Hold your fingers up and out of the way, then slide a serrated knife between the lids and carefully slice through the tomatoes.

CHEESY JALAPEÑO POPPER QUESADILLAS

This ain't your mama's cheese crisp! We took one of our favorite game day dishes and transformed it into the most amazing and hearty cheesy jalapeño popper quesadillas. It is loaded with seasoned beef, jalapeños, bacon and two kinds of cheese. Sierra and I love cheese crisps and quesadillas, but Chad always thought they were not quite flavorful enough. It's no wonder that this spectacular flavorful recipe won Chad over to team quesadilla. Go cheese, GO!

8 oz (227 g) lean ground beef (about 88% lean)

1 medium jalapeño, diced

½ tsp kosher salt

1 tbsp (7 g) Mexican Seasoning Blend (page 160)

¼ cup (60 ml) water

4 oz (112 g) cream cheese, softened and cut into cubes

½ cup (40 g) bacon crumbles or 8 oz (227 g) bacon, cooked and diced

2 cups (240 g) freshly shredded Colby Jack cheese

4 (8-inch [20-cm]) flour tortillas

2 tbsp (30 ml) extra light olive oil (or another flavorless oil)

In a 10-inch (25.4-cm) skillet over medium-high heat, add the ground beef, jalapeño and salt. Cook until the ground beef is cooked through, stirring occasionally, 3 to 5 minutes. Break the beef up with a spatula as it cooks. Add the seasoning and stir until the beef is completely coated. Add the water and cook, stirring, until the water is almost completely evaporated, about 2 minutes.

Pour the beef mixture into a large bowl and top with the cream cheese cubes. Stir until the cream cheese melts into the hot beef mixture. Add the bacon and shredded cheese. Stir until well combined.

Rinse out the skillet and return it to medium heat.

Lay out the tortillas on a clean countertop and add one-fourth of the mixture to each tortilla. Spread the mixture over half of the tortilla and then fold the tortilla in half.

Drizzle the oil into the warm skillet and carefully place 2 quesadillas into the skillet (folded edge against folded edge to make a circle) and cook until golden brown, 2 to 3 minutes. Flip and cook the other side until golden brown, 2 to 3 minutes. Place on a cooling rack while you prepare the remaining quesadillas. Cut the quesadillas in half.

DONNA'S SIMPLE KITCHEN TIP: If you prefer to make your own bacon crumbles, simply lay slices of bacon on a foil-lined baking pan. Place the pan in the cold oven, turn the heat to 400°F (200°C, or gas mark 6) and bake for 15 to 25 minutes. The length of time will vary based on the thickness of your bacon (thick-cut takes longer) and the doneness you prefer (I like mine crispy). Chop up the cooked bacon and refrigerate until ready to use.

CRUNCHY BAKED CHICKEN STRIPS

These crispy, crunchy, oven-fried chicken strips are delightfully moist and tender. The flavorful Parmesan-cornflake coating and juicy chicken are the perfect combination for a quick dinner that is completely irresistible. I have also fried these chicken strips, and they are amazing either way. They remind us of mozzarella sticks, but you know . . . with chicken. What a great twist!

Olive oil cooking spray

¼ cup (30 g) all-purpose flour

2 tsp (12 g) kosher salt, divided

1 tsp freshly ground black pepper

1 large egg, beaten

2 tbsp (30 ml) whole milk

3 cups (75 g) cornflakes

¼ cup (25 g) freshly shredded Parmesan cheese

1 tbsp (3 g) Tuscan-Style Seasoning Blend (page 160)

1½ lb (680 g) chicken tenders (or boneless skinless chicken breasts, cut into strips)

2 tbsp (8 g) chopped fresh Italian parsley

1 recipe 10-Minute Marinara Arrabbiata (page 147)

Preheat the oven to 450°F (230°C, or gas mark 8). Line a baking sheet with aluminum foil and spray liberally with olive oil cooking spray.

In a gallon-size (3.6-L) zip-top plastic bag, combine the flour, 1 teaspoon of the salt and the pepper. Seal and shake the bag to combine; set aside. In a separate gallon-size (3.6-L) zip-top plastic bag, combine the egg and milk. Seal and shake to combine them; set aside. In a third gallon-size (3.6-L) zip-top plastic bag, add the cornflakes, Parmesan cheese, seasoning blend and the remaining 1 teaspoon of salt. Seal the bag and smash the cornflakes into little pieces and then shake the bag until everything is combined; set aside.

Add the chicken to the bag with the flour mixture. Seal the bag and shake it until the chicken is completely coated. Shake off the excess flour and transfer the chicken to the egg mixture one at a time. Seal the bag and shake it until all the strips are well coated in the egg wash. Then, add the chicken one piece at a time to the cornflake mixture. Seal the bag and shake to coat the chicken completely. Press the mixture onto the chicken if you need to, to get a good coating.

Place the coated chicken strips on the prepared baking sheet. Spray the chicken liberally with olive oil spray and bake for 12 to 15 minutes, until crispy and cooked through, turning once halfway through the cooking time and spraying again with olive oil.

Remove the baking sheet from the oven, sprinkle the chicken strips with parsley and serve with the marinara sauce.

DONNA'S SIMPLE KITCHEN TIP: To fry the chicken strips, heat canola oil in a large skillet over medium heat until it reaches 350°F (180°C) on a deep-frying thermometer, 2 to 3 minutes. Add the breaded chicken to the hot oil. Fry for 3 to 4 minutes, until the chicken is a deep golden brown color, and then flip and cook for 2 to 3 minutes longer, until the chicken is cooked through. Make sure the juices run clear.

CRISP APPLE SPINACH SALAD WITH CHICKEN

This light and fresh salad is fully loaded with some of my favorite flavors. It's packed with sweet and tart apples and cranberries, fresh baby spinach, creamy feta cheese, toasted pecans and rotisserie chicken. Then it is topped with a fall-inspired apple cider vinaigrette. I could eat it all year long. In fact, I might just do that.

APPLE CIDER VINAIGRETTE

½ cup (160 g) honey

¼ cup (60 ml) apple cider vinegar

¼ cup (60 ml) fresh lemon juice (about 1 lemon)

2 tbsp (30 g) Dijon mustard

½ cup (120 ml) extra light olive oil

½ tsp kosher salt

½ tsp fresh ground black pepper

APPLE SPINACH SALAD

10 oz (280 g) fresh baby spinach

½ red onion, thinly sliced

1 large Gala apple, thinly sliced

1 large Granny Smith apple, thinly sliced

1 cup (110 g) toasted pecans

½ cup (75 g) crumbled feta cheese

½ cup (60 g) dried cranberries

2–3 lb (908–1362 g) rotisserie chicken, sliced into ¼" (6-mm) strips

To make the vinaigrette, combine the vinaigrette ingredients in an 8-ounce (235-ml) mason jar. Seal and shake the living tar out of it, until well combined. Place in the refrigerator.

To make the salad, in a large salad bowl, combine the spinach, onion, apples, pecans, feta cheese and cranberries. Toss everything with salad tongs to combine. Add the chicken strips on top and pour the dressing over the salad. Toss with salad tongs again.

DONNA'S SIMPLE KITCHEN TIP: If you can't find toasted nuts, you can toss them in a skillet over medium heat and cook for 4 to 5 minutes, swirling them in the pan occasionally, until they are golden brown and fragrant. Don't leave them unattended. Nuts can go from pale to burned in no time flat. Smaller nuts will cook faster, so be sure to keep an eye on them.

PAN-FRIED FIRECRACKER PORK CHOPS

Chicken-fried, tender pork chops with a spectacular crunchy coating are tossed in a Sriracha aioli to create this dynamite dinner inspired by the famous shrimp. These pork chops are moist and tender inside with a double-crisp seasoned chicken-fried coating that will blow your mind. Mexican spices, fried pork chops and Sriracha aioli . . . Who said pork chops had to be boring?

PORK CHOPS

1 large egg

½ cup (120 ml) buttermilk

3 tsp (18 g) kosher salt, divided

1 tbsp (7 g) Mexican Seasoning Blend (page 160), divided

1 cup (120 g) all-purpose flour

½ cup (120 ml) canola oil (or another light-flavored oil for frying)

4 bone-in center-cut pork chops (about ½" [1.3-cm] thick)

1 scallion, chopped

Handful of fresh Italian parsley, chopped

SRIRACHA AIOLI

½ cup (120 g) mayonnaise

4 tsp (20 ml) Sriracha

1 tbsp (20 g) honey

½ tsp garlic powder

¼ tsp kosher salt

To make the pork chops, combine the egg, buttermilk, 2 teaspoons (12 g) of the salt and 1 teaspoon of the Mexican seasoning in a shallow bowl or pie plate and whisk together. Set aside. In a separate shallow bowl or pie plate, combine the flour, remaining 2 teaspoons (4 g) of Mexican seasoning and the remaining 1 teaspoon of salt. Drizzle 2 to 3 tablespoons (30 to 45 ml) of the egg mixture into the flour and work it in with a fork until there are little clumps throughout. This helps develop the extra crunchy bits on the pork chops.

Warm the canola oil in a 10-inch (25.4-cm) skillet over medium heat until hot, 2 to 3 minutes. Place a pork chop in the buttermilk egg mixture and flip to make sure it is completely coated. Dredge the pork chop in the flour mixture, flipping it to make sure it is completely coated in flour. Shake off the excess and transfer it back to the buttermilk mixture again. Yep. We are double-coating these chops! Then back into the flour mixture again. Take the time to press the flour onto the pork chop and then gently shake off the excess. Trust me. The crispy coating is amazing!

Add the pork chops to the hot oil. Fry for 3 to 4 minutes, until the chops are a deep golden brown, then flip and cook for 2 to 3 minutes on the second side. Make sure the juices run clear. Place on a plate.

Meanwhile, to make the aioli, in a medium bowl, combine all of the aioli ingredients and whisk to blend. Pour the sauce over the pork chops right before serving and flip to coat on both sides. Sprinkle with the scallions and parsley. If you need to wait to serve dinner, just hold off on applying the aioli until right before you serve it or the sauce will seep into the crisp coating.

DONNA'S SIMPLE KITCHEN TIP: To make quick work of cleanup, you can combine the buttermilk-egg mixture in a gallon-size (3.6-L) zip-top bag and the flour mixture in another gallon-size (3.6-L) zip-top bag and dip and dredge right out of the bags!

FOUR

SIMPLE APPETIZERS

Parties are my favorite! I absolutely geek out over the planning and shopping. My all-time favorite party has to be the *Ocean's Eleven* casino surprise party I threw for Chad's birthday. Or maybe it's the *Frozen* birthday party for Sierra we had last year. Or, the Elmo party ranks pretty high up there, too. It's hard to choose.

The casino party was the best birthday party Chad has ever had. I had so much fun planning the party and preparing the perfect party favors for about fifty guests. I rented casino tables and set up lighted tents and tables in the backyard. I had some friends help set up the party. It was an absolutely amazing event, but I never realized that I would be so busy with the food that I would spend the entire night in the kitchen. Well, shortly after that things changed.

I started thinking about recipes that I could make and serve in a slow cooker or make ahead and just warm up before serving. That completely changed my party mind-set. The first criteria I look at now is, can I make it ahead or can I buy it? My top party choices are make-ahead or no-fuss recipes.

Slow Cooker Sweet and Spicy Barbecue Wings (page 77) are one of our favorites. Everyone loves wings, especially during game-day parties. These wings are prepared in the slow cooker and finished under the broiler, creating a perfectly tender chicken wing that melts in your mouth with a scrumptious sticky sauce without ever touching a fryer.

Crispy Southern Fried Chicken (page 81) is always a crowd-pleaser! It is tender and juicy with the most amazing flavorful crisp crust. We love this for afternoon parties, family get-togethers, game-day gatherings and also just because it's Tuesday and it's so stinking good. It's a single dip chicken, but you'd never know it! It's perfect to make ahead and serve at room temperature.

Garlic-Parmesan Pizza Pinwheels (page 78) always disappear as fast as you can put them out. Soft and tender garlic-Parmesan bread dough is loaded up with spicy marinara and pepperoni and then baked to golden perfection.

Stacked Cantina Nachos (page 86) are probably my all-time favorite appetizer, although I also enjoy them for lunch and dinner, so I guess you can say they are very adaptable. Completely loaded up with all your favorite nacho toppings, they are perfect for serving a crowd.

Now that I have my party priorities in order, I spend all my time with our friends, family and, of course, the guest of honor. In a world where convenience is king, simple is the reigning queen and it all starts with easy recipes.

SLOW COOKER SWEET AND SPICY BARBECUE WINGS

Slow cooker wings are so tender and juicy they melt in your mouth. You get the best of both worlds with this bold barbecue sauce. The spicy chili pepper paste and the honey and brown sugar come together to create the perfect sweet and spicy coating. After the wings are slow cooked, I broil them in the oven until the glaze is gloriously caramelized and sticky. These wings can be prepped ahead and then warmed in the slow cooker for serving. There's no frying, no mess. Easy stress-free recipes are one of the steps to the ultimate party, because who needs all that extra work anyway? Oh, and no frying means they must be healthier, so you can eat more. Am I right or am I right?

¼ cup (80 g) honey

½ cup (112 g) packed light brown sugar

½ cup (120 g) ketchup

2 tbsp (30 ml) soy sauce

2-3 tbsp (30–45 g) chili pepper paste, to taste

1 tsp kosher salt

2 cloves garlic, minced

3 lb (1.4 kg) fresh chicken wing drumettes*

In a 5-quart (4.5-L) slow cooker on low, add the honey, brown sugar, ketchup, soy sauce, chili pepper, salt and garlic. Stir to combine. Add the chicken wings. Stir until the wings are well-coated. Cover and cook for 1 to 2 hours on high (or 2½ to 3 hours on low), until the wings are cooked through.

Remove the wings from the slow cooker and place on a baking sheet lined with foil.

Transfer the sauce from the slow cooker to a saucepan and bring to a boil over medium-high heat. Cook the sauce until it is thick enough to coat the back of a spoon, 7 to 10 minutes, stirring occasionally. Then slather the thickened sauce over the wings. Broil for 2 to 3 minutes, until the sauce starts to darken and caramelize. And don't leave the oven. Broiling can go from caramelized to burned in a blink, just trust me on this one. Open the oven and brush another layer of sauce on the wings and broil again. Repeat until you have three layers of sauce on the wings. Remove from the oven.

*You can use frozen wings; the cook time will be 2 to 3 hours on high (4 to 6 hours on low).

DONNA'S SIMPLE KITCHEN TIP: I use the "stir-in" chili pepper paste from a tube; it is found in the produce department by the herbs. You can also find chili pepper paste in tubes in the Italian food aisle.

GARLIC-PARMESAN PIZZA PINWHEELS

Pizza is so popular, but these pinwheels are sure to kick up the fun factor! The dough is slightly crisp on the outside and tender inside. It's like unrolling a little piece of heaven wrapped in marinara and ooey gooey cheese. Swoon! Everyone went nuts over these. Sierra loves them anytime she can get them; I mean, hello, they are pizza! The best part is that you can make them ahead and warm them to serve when you are ready, which makes them party-perfect! If you are short on time, you can even substitute store-bought pizza dough. Easy party + fun food = happy mama!

4 tbsp (56 g) unsalted butter, melted

1 recipe Garlic-Herb Parmesan Pizza Dough (page 159)

1 cup (240 ml) 10-Minute Marinara Arrabbiata (page 147)

2 cups (240 g) freshly shredded mozzarella cheese

40 slices pepperoni

½ tsp dried parsley

¼ tsp kosher salt

1 recipe 5-Ingredient Alfredo Sauce (page 155), optional

Preheat the oven to 350°F (180°C, or gas mark 4). Butter a baking sheet with the melted butter. Reserve the remaining butter. Set aside.

On a lightly floured countertop, roll the dough into a 12 x 18-inch (30.5 x 46-cm) rectangle. Spread ½ to 1 cup (120 to 240 ml) of marinara over the dough, leaving a 1-inch (2.5-cm) border on the top edge. Sprinkle the cheese over the sauce and make rows of pepperoni on top of the cheese. You'll want to leave about 1 inch (2.5 cm) or so between each row.

Starting at the long edge nearest you, fold the edge of the dough on top of itself and begin tightly rolling the dough away from you, pinching the pepperoni slices into the roll if they try to escape as you go. Use the last 1 inch (2.5 cm) of clean dough to seal the roll, pressing gently to keep it closed. Cut the roll in half and then cut those halves in half, giving you 4 logs. Cut each of those logs into 3 pinwheels, giving you 12 pinwheels total. See, math class did come in handy after all, who knew?

Arrange the pinwheels cut side up on the baking sheet and spread them out so they are not touching. Bake for 20 minutes, or until they are golden brown and cooked through.

Meanwhile, combine the remaining butter, parsley and salt in a small bowl. Stir together with a pastry brush or spoon. Brush the top and sides of the baked pinwheels with the butter mixture. Serve with the remaining marinara and the Alfredo sauce, if desired.

DONNA'S SIMPLE KITCHEN TIP: These freeze wonderfully. Simply allow them to cool to room temperature after baking. Store in a gallon-size (3.6-L) zip-top bag in the freezer. When you are ready to eat, just thaw them and bake at 350°F (180°C, or gas mark 4) for 10 minutes, or until warmed through.

CRISPY SOUTHERN FRIED CHICKEN

Southern-style buttermilk fried chicken is juicy and tender with a divinely flavorful crust and little crisp bits of coating that will make your mouth sing! The magic in the coating is buttermilk drizzled into the spiced flour mixture to help build that crisp crust in just one dip. How easy is that? Now let's get down to the real business . . . the spices. They are aromatic with a hint of smokiness and heat. Fried chicken is awesome for picnics, lunch and parties because it is delicious served at room temperature, so you can make it the day before and refrigerate until 30 to 60 minutes before you are ready to serve. I use this recipe to make chicken nuggets and chicken strips, too. The more the merrier, am I right?

3 lb (1.4 kg) chicken drumsticks

1¾ cups (410 ml) low-fat buttermilk, divided

4 tsp (24 g) kosher salt, divided

2 tsp (4 g) freshly ground black pepper

Peanut oil, for frying

1 cup (120 g) all-purpose flour

2 tbsp (14 g) paprika

2 tbsp (6 g) Tuscan-Style Seasoning Blend (page 160)

1 tbsp (6 g) white pepper

DONNA'S SIMPLE KITCHEN TIP: If the chicken is browned but the juices are still pink, you can bake the drumsticks in a 325°F (170°C, or gas mark 3) oven until cooked through.

Rinse the chicken and pat dry. Combine the chicken and 1½ cups (355 ml) of the buttermilk in a gallon-size (3.6-L) zip-top bag. Seal the bag and shake to combine. Marinate the chicken in the fridge for 1 hour and up to overnight, flipping once.

Remove the chicken from the buttermilk and shake off the excess. Place the chicken on a wire rack set over a baking sheet. Season both sides of the chicken with 2 teaspoons (12 g) of the salt and the freshly ground pepper. Let the chicken sit at room temperature for 30 minutes. If the chicken is too cold, it will affect that delicious crispy coating!

Fill a 12-inch (30.5-cm) cast-iron skillet about one-third of the way up with oil and heat the oil to over medium heat until it reaches 350°F (180°C) on a deep-frying thermometer.

Meanwhile, combine the flour, paprika, seasoning blend, white pepper and remaining 2 teaspoons (12 g) of salt in a gallon-size (3.6-L) zip-top bag. Slowly drizzle the remaining ¼ cup (60 ml) of buttermilk into the flour as you wiggle and shake the bag to create multiple little clumps. Work the flour with your fingertips; this will help give your chicken those crispy bits that everyone loves so much.

Add one piece of chicken to the bag at a time; hold the bag closed with one hand and shake until well-coated, pressing the coating onto the chicken if needed. Shake off the excess flour and place the chicken on a plate to rest. Repeat until all of the chicken is coated.

Once the oil reaches 350°F (177°C), use tongs to place half of the chicken drumsticks into the oil and cover the pan (I use a baking sheet). Keep the oil at about 325°F (170°C). Cook for 6 minutes, covered. Flip the chicken and cover again. Cook for 6 minutes longer, or until the chicken coating is browned and the juices run clear when you poke the chicken with a fork. Repeat with the second batch of chicken, bringing the oil up to temperature in between batches.

Meanwhile, wash the wire rack. Remove the chicken from the oil and place it on the wire rack set over a baking sheet to cool. Allow it to rest for 10 minutes. Fried chicken is amazing at room temperature.

JALAPEÑO CHEDDAR PRETZEL TWISTS

Here, soft and chewy, buttery pretzel twists are speckled with spicy jalapeños and loaded with tangy cheddar cheese for the perfect flavor combination. These, my friends, are next level pretzels for sure! They are a game-day tradition around here, and completely addictive. The pretzels can be made ahead and rewarmed, which makes them perfect in our book. They come together in just about 45 minutes and are pretty easy to make. Mix it, twist it, bake it, eat it!

Nonstick cooking spray (optional)

1¼ cups (295 ml) warm beer (110°–120°F [43°–49°C])

2¼ tsp (7 g) active dry yeast

2 tbsp (24 g) sugar

3½–4 cups (420–480 g) all-purpose flour, as needed

1 tsp kosher salt

2 jalapeños, seeded and minced

2 cups (240 g) fresh finely shredded sharp cheddar cheese

4 cups (940 ml) hot water

¼ cup (50 g) baking soda

1 large egg

2 tbsp (30 ml) cool water

Pretzel salt (or coarse salt)

2 tbsp (30 ml) melted butter

1 recipe Jalapeño Spinach Cheese Dip (optional, page 89)

DONNA'S SIMPLE KITCHEN TIP: If you are sensitive to alcohol, you can substitute the beer with water.

Check out the 40-Minute Dinner Rolls (page 148) for tips on making dough without a stand mixer.

Preheat the oven to 450°F (230°C, or gas mark 8). Line a baking sheet with parchment paper or spray with nonstick cooking spray.

Pour the warm beer into the bowl of a stand mixer fitted with a dough hook, sprinkle the yeast on top and add the sugar. Stir to mix everything together. Allow the yeast to bloom for 3 to 5 minutes. Once it is aromatic and foamy, it is ready. Add 3½ cups (420 g) of the flour and the salt to the mixer. Knead the dough for about 3 minutes, until the dough comes together into a ball. Add the jalapeños and cheese and mix until combined, about 1 minute. The dough should be tacky, not sticky. When you touch the dough with your fingertips and pull them away, they should not take any dough with them. Add more flour, 1 tablespoon (8 g) at a time, as needed to make it tacky.

Meanwhile, fill a large bowl with the hot water and baking soda. In a separate small bowl, beat the egg and cool water with a fork to make the egg wash. Set the bowls aside.

Place the dough on an unfloured countertop and form the dough into a ball. Cut the ball in half and in half again to quarter the ball of dough. Roll each quarter into a log and cut the log into 3 equal pieces. When you are done you will have 12 pieces. Roll each piece into a rope 18 to 24 inches (46 to 61 cm) long. Fold a rope in half, making two ropes the same length. Twist the ropes together and then pinch the bottom together and tuck the edge underneath. Place the pretzel twist on the prepared baking sheet. Repeat until all 12 twists are on the sheet.

Transfer 2 or 3 pretzel twists at a time into the hot water mixture for 30 to 45 seconds. Remove the twists from the water with a slotted spoon and place them back on the prepared baking sheet. Repeat until all of the twists are on the baking sheet. Re-twist any pretzels that did not cooperate. Brush the egg wash onto each twist and sprinkle with the pretzel salt.

Bake for 8 to 10 minutes, until the tops are browned. Brush the pretzel twists with the melted butter. Serve with the cheese dip, if desired.

SLOW COOKER BOURBON BROWN SUGAR MEATBALLS

What's better than tender, juicy meatballs cooked in the most splendid bourbon brown sugar barbecue sauce? It is a little hot, a little sweet and perfectly smoky. It's a superb party recipe that will leave you hoping for leftovers. These are perfect for dinner, too—we love them served over rice! You literally mix the ingredients and toss them in the slow cooker. The magic happens while they cook. The scrumptious sauce cooks into the meatballs until you have thick and rich, tasty glazed meatballs to serve partygoers. With easy prep they are perfect for a simple party or fabulous for a fancy get-together. Serve them right out of the slow cooker or put them on a tray with toothpicks. Hide the forks until you are ready to serve or they will disappear!

½ cup (112 g) packed light brown sugar

½ cup (120 g) ketchup

¼ cup (60 ml) bourbon

1 tbsp (15 ml) apple cider vinegar

1 tbsp (15 g) Dijon mustard

1 tsp garlic powder

1-2 tbsp (15–30 g) chili paste, to taste

1 recipe Italian Herb Baked Meatballs (page 160)

In a small mixing bowl, combine the brown sugar, ketchup, bourbon, vinegar, mustard, garlic powder and chili paste and whisk until combined.

Place the meatballs into the slow cooker and pour the sauce over the top. Stir to combine everything. Cook for 2 to 3 hours on high (or 4 to 6 hours on low).

DONNA'S SIMPLE KITCHEN TIPS: If you prefer perfectly round meatballs, you can bake the meatballs before adding them to the slow cooker or you can add the meatballs and sauce to the slow cooker and cook them together. Be sure to stir carefully until they are cooked through.

If you are sensitive to alcohol, you can substitute cola for the bourbon.

STACKED CANTINA NACHOS

I have yet to meet a plate of nachos that I didn't like, and to be honest, I would just as soon sit down to a gloriously cheesy plate of nachos rather than dinner . . . or even dessert (gasp). These nachos are stacked to the roof! It all starts with crunchy tortilla chips, topped with seasoned beef, creamy refried beans and tons of ooey gooey cheese with spicy jalapeños. We loaded on my favorite fixin's, too. Chunky salsa and guacamole really bring this all together. These are game-day and party perfect! Just prep them before the party and toss them in the oven right before it starts. It's like a visit to your favorite Mexican restaurant but in the comfort of your own home. Mmm hmm, doing the happy dance!

1 lb (454 g) lean ground beef

1 tsp kosher salt, divided

2 tbsp (14 g) Mexican Seasoning Blend (page 160)

¼ cup (60 ml) water

1 (1-lb [454-g]) bag tortilla chips

1 (16-oz [454-g]) can refried beans

1 cup (120 g) freshly shredded Colby Jack cheese

½ cup (68 g) pickled jalapeños

½ cup (120 ml) Everything Cheese Sauce (page 144), warmed

½ cup (120 g) Restaurant-Style Chunky Salsa (page 151), strained

¼ cup (60 g) guacamole

¼ cup (60 g) sour cream

Preheat the oven to 350°F (180°C, or gas mark 4).

Warm a 10-inch (25.4-cm) skillet over medium-high heat. Once you can feel the heat when you hold your hand 6 inches (15 cm) above the skillet, add the ground beef and ½ teaspoon of the salt. Cook the beef until it is cooked through, using a spatula to break up the beef as it cooks, 5 to 7 minutes. Drain the excess drippings if necessary (I had very few drippings).

Sprinkle the spice blend and the remaining ½ teaspoon of salt over the beef. Stir everything together until the beef is completely coated with the seasoning. Add the water and cook the seasoned beef until the water is mostly evaporated, stirring occasionally. When it is done, set it aside.

Fill a 9 x 13-inch (23 x 33-cm) baking dish with one layer of tortilla chips. Top the chips with half of each of the refried beans, seasoned beef, Colby Jack cheese and jalapeños. Add a second layer of chips and repeat the toppings. Add a smaller third layer in the center. Bake the nachos until the cheese is melted, about 10 minutes.

Drizzle the nachos with the warm cheese sauce, then spoon the salsa over the top. Add dollops of guacamole and drizzle with the sour cream.

DONNA'S SIMPLE KITCHEN TIP: Zip-top bags are perfect for drizzling. Just scoop your desired topping into the bag, squeeze the air out and push the filling to the corner. Cut a tiny bit off the corner of the bag. The more you cut off, the bigger the drizzle. So start small, and you can always cut more. Squeeze the bag and drizzle out the topping.

JALAPEÑO SPINACH CHEESE DIP

We love game-day eats, and this spicy cheese dip is at the top of the list! It is rich, creamy and perfectly cheesy with just the right touch of spinach. A luscious pepper Jack cheese sauce with a sprinkling of onions, jalapeño and tomatoes has just enough heat to wake up your taste buds. It is wildly popular at my house. Every time I put a bowl of this cheese dip out, our guests gather around until it's gone. It is truly a people magnet and the fact that it comes together in one pan in just about 20 minutes makes it party perfect. Yay, cheese!

1 Roma tomato, seeded and diced

¼ medium white onion, minced

2 jalapeño peppers, seeded and diced

4 tbsp (56 g) unsalted butter

1 tsp kosher salt

4 tbsp (30 g) all-purpose flour

2 cups (470 ml) whole milk

4 cups (480 g) fresh finely shredded pepper Jack cheese

2 oz (56 g) frozen spinach, thawed and squeezed dry

1 recipe Jalapeño Cheddar Pretzel Twists (page 82), optional

Reserve a sprinkling of tomato, onion and jalapeño for garnish.

Add the butter to a small saucepan over medium heat. Add the remaining onion and jalapeño and the salt. Cook until the onions are softened, 3 to 4 minutes, and then sprinkle the flour over the vegetables. Stir until everything is coated really well. Cook for about 1 minute to cook out the floury taste. Add the milk and cook, stirring, until bubbles just start breaking the surface. Remove the pot from the heat and sprinkle the cheese into the saucepan a handful at a time. Stir the sauce until the cheese melts and then add another handful. Continue stirring until the cheese dip is completely smooth. Stir in the spinach and the remaining tomatoes. Sprinkle with the reserved tomato, onion and jalapeño to garnish.

Serve with chips or the pretzel twists.

DONNA'S SIMPLE KITCHEN TIP: To keep the sauce warm until ready to serve, warm over low heat and add extra milk as necessary to keep the sauce from thickening up.

SPICY ITALIAN PRETZEL BOMBS

These pretzel bombs are a spectacular fusion of a spicy Italian sub sandwich and a soft pretzel. They come together easily with the help of frozen dinner-roll dough balls and can be made ahead and rewarmed for your party. Can you imagine? Deli sliced ham, flavorful cured salami, spicy smoked pepperoni and sharp aged provolone, stuffed inside a soft salty pretzel with roasted red peppers and pepperoncini to create the most sensational pretzel bomb? It truly is a flavor explosion unlike anything you have ever tried!

Nonstick cooking spray (optional)

24 frozen dinner-roll dough balls

1 large egg

2 tbsp (30 ml) water

All-purpose flour, for sprinkling

4 oz (112 g) sliced Genoa salami

4 oz (112 g) sliced pepperoni

4 oz (112 g) sliced deli ham

8 oz (227 g) sliced aged provolone cheese

½ cup (90 g) roasted red peppers

½ cup (60 g) pepperoncini rings, plus 3 tbsp (45 ml) liquid from jar

½ tsp crushed red pepper flakes

¼ cup (50 g) baking soda

Pretzel salt (or coarse salt)

DONNA'S SIMPLE KITCHEN TIP: When rolling dough, make sure you cannot see through the dough. If you have any tears or can't seal the dough, tap your fingertips in flour, tap on any tears and roll again.

Preheat the oven to 450°F (230°C, or gas mark 8). Line a baking sheet with parchment paper or spray it with cooking spray.

Place 12 frozen dinner-roll balls on a microwave-safe plate and heat on defrost for about 2 minutes (or until the dough is still cold, but no longer frozen). Repeat with the remaining 12 dough balls.

In a small bowl, beat the egg and water with a fork. Set aside. Sprinkle a clean countertop with flour.

Chop all of the deli meats, cheese, roasted red peppers and pepperoncini into bite-size pieces (¼ to ½ inch [6 to 13 mm] each). Place all of the pieces into a large bowl and add the liquid from the pepperoncini jar and the red pepper flakes. Toss to combine. Set aside.

Flatten each dough ball into a circle, about 3 inches (7.6 cm) across. You can use a rolling pin, or you can pull the dough around the edges like you are making a mini pizza. Add about 2 tablespoons (20 g) of the spicy Italian mixture to the center of your dough. Carefully pull each side over the center to create a "package." Pinch the edges together to seal and then roll the dough into a ball. Set the pretzel bomb aside and repeat until you have 24 stuffed dough balls.

Bring a 4-quart (3.6-L) saucepan of water to a boil over medium-high heat. Carefully add the baking soda to the boiling water, a sprinkle at a time. It will foam up, and the foam is boiling hot, so don't touch it. Trust me on this one. Place the dough balls into the boiling water a few at a time, using a slotted spoon. After 30 seconds, remove them with the spoon. Place them on the prepared baking sheet, not touching. Repeat until all of the bombs have had a boiling water bath.

Brush each bomb with the egg wash and sprinkle with the pretzel salt. Bake the pretzel bombs for 8 to 10 minutes, until the tops are browned. The gooey cheese may escape some of your pretzel bombs. That is a beautiful thing! Scoop all that cheesy goodness up onto the plate and serve. Your guests will go crazy over them.

CHEESY BUFFALO CHICKEN TAQUITOS

Buffalo chicken is the consummate game-day food, and this fun twist on the classic will knock your socks off. These baked taquitos are crisp on the outside and rich and creamy on the inside with a true flavor explosion. A combination of ranch, buffalo sauce and tons of Colby Jack cheese are loaded up in a tortilla and baked to golden brown perfection. They are an awesome make-ahead party option. You can make them in advance and bake them before you serve. This recipe gives a little heat and a lot of zing, making them a huge crowd-pleaser! Everyone devours these so fast. I make double batches so I can pull them out of the freezer for a quick lunch or dinner anytime. Now that's my kind of cooking!

Nonstick cooking spray

2 oz (56 g) cream cheese, softened

¼ cup (60 ml) ranch dressing

12 oz (340 g) cooked shredded chicken

½ cup (120 ml) Buffalo wing sauce

2 cups (240 g) freshly shredded Colby Jack cheese

2 tbsp (6 g) chopped chives

18–36 (6" [15-cm]) flour or corn tortillas

Kosher salt

2 tbsp (8 g) chopped fresh Italian parsley

Preheat the oven to 425°F (220°C, or gas mark 7). Line 2 baking sheets with aluminum foil and lightly coat with cooking spray. Set aside.

In a large bowl, combine the cream cheese and ranch dressing and stir until blended. Add the chicken, wing sauce, Colby Jack cheese and chives and stir until well-combined.

Lay out 4 tortillas at a time and add a heaping 1 tablespoon (15 g) of the mixture to the lower one-third of the tortilla. This will make approximately 36 taquitos. This amount works best with the corn tortillas, as adding more causes the tortillas to break. Flour tortillas will hold 2 tablespoons (30 g) of the mixture and make about 18 taquitos.

Roll the taquito tightly without tearing the tortilla. Place the taquitos seam side down on the baking sheet and repeat until the baking sheet is full, being careful not to allow the taquitos to touch. If the tortillas are tearing, microwave a few at a time, for about 20 seconds, with a wet paper towel on top. This will help make them more pliable. If the taquitos are unrolling, add a dab of buffalo chicken mixture to the inside end of the taquito and gently press down to seal.

Liberally spray the taquitos with cooking spray and sprinkle with salt. Bake for 15 to 20 minutes, until the tortillas are crisp and the ends begin to brown. Top with the chopped parsley.

DONNA'S SIMPLE KITCHEN TIP: To freeze for later use, prepare the taquitos as described, but do not bake. Place the taquitos on the baking sheet in the freezer. Allow the taquitos to freeze solid, 1 to 2 hours. Once frozen, place them into a gallon-size (3.6-L) zip-top freezer bag and store them until ready to use. They keep well for 6 months. To prepare the frozen taquitos, preheat the oven to 425°F (220°C, or gas mark 7) and bake for 20 minutes, or until the tortillas are crisp and the ends are beginning to brown.

HOT HAM AND CHEESE PARTY SLIDERS

One of Chad's favorite sandwiches has always been a hot ham and cheese. You know, there is a science to the perfect ham and cheese. It is all about the right ratio of ham to cheese to bread, and boy, did we nail it. We layer honey-baked ham with nutty Swiss cheese on soft and tender sliders and top it with an unexpected sweet and tangy sauce. Then they are baked until the ham is hot and the cheese is gloriously melted. They come out of the oven browned on top and slightly crisp on the edges and bottom. When we went to Iowa for Chad's high school reunion, he took me straight to his favorite fast food restaurant to indulge in a hot ham and cheese sandwich. This slider is a nod to that old-school favorite of Chad's, although we totally kicked it up a notch for game day. They are excellent to prep ahead and then toss in the oven right before you are ready to serve.

1 (12-ct) package white slider rolls

1½ lb (680 g) thinly sliced good-quality Swiss cheese

1½ lb (680 g) thinly sliced honey-baked ham

3 tbsp (42 g) unsalted butter, melted

1 tbsp (20 g) good-quality honey

½ tbsp (6 g) Dijon mustard

½ tbsp (4 g) sesame seeds

⅛ tsp onion powder

Preheat the oven to 350°F (180°C, or gas mark 4). Line a baking sheet with foil.

Separate the rolls and place the bottoms on the baking sheet so they are not touching. Place half of the Swiss cheese slices on the bottom rolls. Top with the ham and layer the remaining Swiss cheese over the ham. Place the tops on each slider.

Combine the melted butter, honey, mustard, sesame seeds and onion powder in a small bowl. Brush 1 teaspoon of sauce on the top of each slider. Use the entire amount. Tent the sliders with foil to help steam them. Bake for 15 minutes. Remove the foil and bake for 5 minutes longer, or until the cheese is bubbly and melted.

DONNA'S SIMPLE KITCHEN TIP: You can also use 40-Minute Milk and Honey Dinner Rolls (page 148).

FIVE

SENSATIONAL SOUPS

When I first fell in love with cooking, it was the ability to create incredible flavors that most excited me about getting into the kitchen. Granted, I started out enjoying baking, but once I realized that with cooking I could go off script and break all the rules, I was on a mission. Soup recipes are the perfect place to experiment with building layers of rich flavor.

We are a divided house when it comes to soups. Chad loves brothy soups and I love stick-to-your-ribs soups. I figure, if I am going to eat soup, it should be hearty enough to be a meal. To keep everyone happy, I make both brothy and hearty soups, and so lucky for you, that means you get recipes for both.

Hearty Beef Soup (page 99) is the best beef soup *ever*! Perfectly seared tender chunks of beef in a rich red wine beef broth with vegetables. You just can't help but linger over every bite. It is our favorite soup of all time. It blows up on our website all year long as millions of people flock to our site to get the recipe. It's the ultimate meal in a bowl.

Chicken Alfredo Tortellini Soup (page 112) is like your favorite chicken Alfredo with vegetables in a rich and velvety soup. It is warm and comforting and utterly happy-dance inducing!

Fire-Roasted Tomato Basil Soup (page 111) is another one of Chad's favorites. I have been making a long cooking version of this soup for years, but it has never been this easy or this delicious! Slow Cooker Chicken and Herb Dumplings (page 107) gets rave reviews from everyone who has ever tried it. It's a simple recipe of shredded chicken, vegetables and light and fluffy herb dumplings that comes together in the slow cooker.

Fire-Roasted Roadhouse Chili (page 103) comes together in 15 minutes with just six ingredients and it is our go-to chili recipe. It's thick and rich, truly a beefy, stick-to-your-ribs chili that your family will love.

Grab your spoon and get your soup on!

HEARTY BEEF SOUP

Look no further: This is the best-ever beef soup, with tender, juicy chunks of seared beef that melt in your mouth and a glorious, rich red wine broth. It's loaded with tender potatoes and carrots. Chad asks for this soup all the time and then paces around the kitchen in anticipation waiting for it to be ready. Is it done yet? Luckily, it has only 20 minutes of active cooking time. It is definitely a member of the clean-plate club, because this soup is so good, you'll lick the bowl clean!

2 lb (908 g) beef chuck roast

¼ cup (30 g) all-purpose flour

1 tsp paprika

1 tsp coarsely ground black pepper

2 tsp (12 g) kosher salt, divided

2 tbsp (30 ml) extra virgin olive oil

2 tbsp (28 g) unsalted butter

1 shallot, diced

3 cloves garlic, minced

1 cup (235 ml) Cabernet Sauvignon

4 cups (940 ml) beef stock

2 tsp (10 ml) Worcestershire sauce

1 tbsp (3 g) Tuscan-Style Seasoning Blend (page 160)

4 cups (600 g) chopped red potatoes, cut into ½" (1.3-cm) pieces

3 cups (360 g) chopped baby carrots, cut into ½" (1.3-cm) pieces

Chopped fresh Italian parsley, for garnish (optional)

Trim the hard fat (which does not melt during the cooking process) and silver skin (white and silvery looking) from the beef and cut into 1 to 1½-inch (2.5 to 3.8-cm) cubes. It takes about 5 minutes, but don't skip this step. It is sooo worth it.

Combine the flour, paprika, pepper and 1 teaspoon of the salt in a gallon-size (3.6-L) zip-top bag. Seal the bag and shake to combine the flour and spices. Add all of the beef cubes and then seal and shake until well coated.

Warm a 6-quart (5.4-L) Dutch oven (or heavy-bottomed pot) over medium-high heat. Once you can feel the heat when you hold your hand 6 inches (15 cm) above the pot, add the olive oil and butter. When the butter is melted, remove the beef from the flour and shake it gently to remove the loose flour. Place the coated beef in the pan, one piece at a time, and brown on all sides. When you add the beef to the pan it will sizzle and hiss. If it doesn't make a big fuss, the pan is not hot enough. Cook the beef in two batches, about half each time. Turn the pieces until all of the sides are browned and then remove them and place on a plate.

Once all of the beef is browned, add the shallot and garlic to the pan and cook them until the shallots are translucent, about 3 minutes. Add the wine and deglaze the pan by scraping up the browned bits at the bottom. Add the beef stock, Worcestershire, seasoning blend and the remaining 1 teaspoon of salt. Stir to combine everything. Return the beef to the pot, cover and bring to a boil. Reduce the heat to a simmer and cook for 40 minutes.

Add the potatoes and carrots and stir to combine. Cover and simmer for 40 to 50 minutes, or until the vegetables are fork-tender. Taste the broth and add more salt to taste (mine was perfect). Garnish with fresh parsley, if desired.

DONNA'S SIMPLE KITCHEN TIPS: The best cuts of meat to use for this soup are chuck roast, chuck shoulder, chuck-eye roast and top chuck. I do not recommend using beef stew meat.

If you are sensitive to alcohol, you can substitute the Cabernet Sauvignon with beef stock or grape, pomegranate or cranberry juice.

RESTAURANT-STYLE LEMON CHICKEN ORZO SOUP

This comforting chicken soup with a bright lemony broth is loaded with fresh vegetables and a sprinkling of pasta to keep it light. Bursting with citrus flavor and tender chunks of chicken, sweet carrots, baby spinach and a touch of orzo pasta, this is my perfect anytime soup, especially after I may have eaten a few too many delicious desserts. It's all about balance, right?

8 cups (1.9 L) reduced-sodium chicken stock

1 lb (454 g) boneless skinless chicken breast, cut into bite-size pieces

2 lemons, 1 lemon juiced and 1 lemon sliced

1 cup (120 g) baby carrots, sliced into coins

2 cloves garlic, minced

1 tbsp (15 g) reduced-sodium chicken base (or bouillon)

1 tsp Tuscan-Style Seasoning Blend (page 160)

1 tsp onion powder

1 tsp kosher salt, divided

2 oz (56 g) uncooked orzo pasta

1 tsp freshly ground black pepper

3 oz (84 g) fresh baby spinach leaves

In a large pot over medium-high heat, combine the chicken stock, chicken, lemon juice, carrots, garlic, chicken base, seasoning blend, onion powder and ½ teaspoon of the salt. Cook for 5 minutes and then add the orzo. Bring to a boil and cook for 8 minutes longer, and then add the pepper.

Taste for seasoning. Add the remaining ½ teaspoon of salt, if desired. Sprinkle with the spinach. Stir to combine. Garnish with the lemon slices.

DONNA'S SIMPLE KITCHEN TIP: Orzo and rice have a tendency to continue to absorb liquid, leaving a soup brothless. If you are not serving the soup immediately, it is best to prepare the orzo or rice separately and add it in when you serve the soup.

FIRE-ROASTED ROADHOUSE CHILI

Everyone has a chili recipe, but I can tell you this one is so good and so easy it's the only recipe we ever use. This chili is a meat lover's dream, with tons of beef, it's bursting with smoky flavors and it has just enough heat to make you feel the warmth. The fire-roasted tomatoes and jalapeños add a long-cooked flavor to this simple recipe, which is ready in 15 minutes. I actually whipped up this chili for the first time one day when we had friends over and I wanted to make a quick comforting lunch that everyone would love, and oh boy, did I ever succeed. There wasn't a drop left. Chad says, "This is the kind of recipe that makes me wish I had a second stomach." I couldn't agree more.

2 lb (908 g) lean ground beef (85–88% lean)

1 tsp kosher salt, divided

1 tsp crushed red pepper flakes, or to taste

2 (14.5-oz [410-ml]) cans fire-roasted diced tomatoes with garlic

2 (15.5-oz [440-g]) cans chili beans (I used S&W)

½ (4-oz [112-g]) can fire-roasted diced jalapeños, or to taste

Heat a 4-quart (3.6-L) saucepan over medium-high heat. Once you can feel the heat when you hold your hand 6 inches (15 cm) above the pot, add the beef, ½ teaspoon of the salt and the red pepper flakes. Break up the meat with a wooden spoon as it cooks. Continue cooking just until the beef is cooked through, stirring occasionally, 5 to 7 minutes. If there is any liquid left in the pan you can drain it out, if you prefer. However, a few tablespoons of drippings adds great flavor.

Add the tomatoes, beans and jalapeños. Stir the chili and simmer for 5 minutes. Taste for seasoning and add the remaining ½ teaspoon salt, if desired.

DONNA'S SIMPLE KITCHEN TIPS: Using fire-roasted tomatoes in place of crushed or diced tomatoes gives recipes a depth of flavor that makes you think it cooked all day long.

You can use diced green chiles in place of the fire-roasted jalapeños for a milder flavor.

SERVES 8

FRENCH ONION MEATBALL SOUP

I always loved the idea of French onion soup, but I never truly enjoyed it until I decided to add in my favorite meatballs, which make it hearty, more like a meal. It is luxurious, comforting and utterly satisfying. The wine and beef stock come together with the sweet onions, herbs and spices to create a spectacular base, and the hearty meatballs knock it out of the park. Topped with a scrumptious cheese bread, this soup is a hit with everyone. I mean, how could it not be?

4 tbsp (56 g) unsalted butter

4 lb (1.9 kg) sweet onions

1 recipe Italian Herb Baked Meatballs, uncooked (page 143)

2 tbsp (16 g) all-purpose flour

1 cup (235 ml) Cabernet Sauvignon

8 cups (1.9 L) reduced-sodium beef stock

6 cloves garlic, minced

2 tsp (3 g) dried thyme

2 tsp (12 g) kosher salt (more to taste)

1 tsp black pepper

1 tbsp (15 ml) Worcestershire sauce

1 French baguette, cut into 16 (1" [2.5-cm]) slices

8 slices provolone cheese, cut in half

Melt the butter in a 5-quart (4.5-L) Dutch oven or heavy-bottomed pot over medium-high heat. Working next to the stove, halve and thinly slice the onions. Add them to the pot as you slice each onion. Stir the onions to coat them in butter. Cook until they are lightly caramelized, stirring occasionally, 10 to 15 minutes.

Meanwhile, using a 1-tablespoon (14-g) scoop, portion the meatballs into small balls.

Once the onions are caramelized, sprinkle them with the flour and stir until no flour clumps remain. Cook for 1 minute to cook out the floury taste. Add the wine to deglaze the pan. Scrape the browned bits off the bottom of the pan and bring the wine to a boil for about 3 minutes. Add the beef stock, garlic, thyme, salt, pepper and Worcestershire and stir to combine. Cover and bring to a boil.

Add the meatballs to the soup, distributing them evenly around the pot. Cover and boil for 10 minutes, or until the meatballs are cooked through. Taste and add salt as necessary.

Meanwhile, preheat the oven to broil. Place the French bread slices on a baking sheet and top each slice with half a slice of Provolone cheese. Broil until the cheese is melted and bubbly, 1 to 2 minutes. Serve each bowl with 2 slices of cheesy bread.

DONNA'S SIMPLE KITCHEN TIPS: When cooking onions, radial slices hold up best. Start by cutting the stem and the root end off the onion. Cut the onion in half from the root to the stem. Remove the skin, turn the onion with the stem end facing you and cut from pole to pole. Start on the side and turn your knife to get the radial cut. This will give you even onion slices.

If you are sensitive to alcohol, you can use 1 cup (235 ml) beef stock in place of the wine.

SLOW COOKER CHICKEN AND HERB DUMPLINGS

Chicken and dumplings is the perfect comfort food, and this one is a family favorite. The base is a robust, rich and creamy chicken soup with tender bites of shredded chicken and fresh vegetables. It's topped with the most amazing fluffy herb dumplings. We sent a pot of these chicken and dumplings over to my mother-in-law's house and it was so good, she called for the recipe. Family tested, Gigi approved!

CHICKEN

3 lb (1.4 kg) boneless skinless chicken breasts

8 oz (227 g) baby carrots, each cut into 4 thick coins

1 tbsp (18 g) kosher salt, divided

2 tsp (3 g) dried thyme

1 tsp onion powder

2 bay leaves

4 cups (940 ml) reduced-sodium chicken stock

1 cup (235 ml) half-and-half

½ cup (60 g) cornstarch

2 tsp (4 g) freshly ground black pepper, or to taste

1 cup (130 g) frozen peas

2 tsp (1 g) dried parsley

DUMPLINGS

2 cups (240 g) all-purpose flour

1 tbsp (12 g) baking powder

1 tbsp (14 g) sugar

1 tsp kosher salt

4 tbsp (56 g) unsalted butter, at room temperature

1 cup (235 ml) whole milk

1 tsp dried thyme

1 tsp dried parsley

To make the chicken, place the chicken breasts on the bottom of your slow cooker (I like to use a 6-quart [5.4-L] for this recipe). Sprinkle in the carrots, 2 teaspoons (12 g) of the salt, thyme, onion powder and bay leaves. Pour the chicken stock over the top and stir to combine the soup. Cover and cook for 3 hours on high (or 6 hours on low).

Meanwhile, to make the dumplings, combine all the dumpling ingredients in a medium bowl. Mix with a spoon until the dough comes together; set aside.

Add the half-and-half and cornstarch to a mason jar. Seal and shake the living tar out of it, until the mixture is smooth, to create a slurry. Set aside.

Remove the 2 bay leaves from the slow cooker and discard. Remove the chicken and place on a plate. Re-cover the slow cooker. Use two forks to shred the chicken (or use the chicken shredding tip on page 18) and add it back to the slow cooker along with any juices remaining on the plate. Add the pepper, peas and parsley to the slow cooker. Pour the slurry through a sieve into the slow cooker. Press any lumps through with a spoon. Stir to combine.

Add the dumplings to the slow cooker by the tablespoon (14 g). Cover and reduce the heat to low. Cook for 1 hour. Do not take the lid off until it's finished cooking. Taste for seasoning and add the remaining 1 teaspoon of salt if needed.

DONNA'S SIMPLE KITCHEN TIP: Half-and-half is simply half cream and half milk, a combination you can use instead if you don't have half-and-half on hand.

RESTAURANT-STYLE BROCCOLI CHEESE SOUP

Broccoli and carrots in a creamy and luxurious smooth cheddar cheese sauce make for my all-time favorite soup. The bold cheese flavor with the added freshness from the broccoli is purely glorious. You can puree it like that restaurant around the corner, but I love it chunky. Since I was a kid, broccoli cheese soup has always been my favorite. Trust me, it wasn't the broccoli that drew me in. Actually, it was the only way I would eat broccoli without a fuss. Now, you can't keep me away from it. Oh, the power of cheese!

4 tbsp (56 g) unsalted butter

½ medium yellow onion, chopped

1 cup (120 g) diced carrot

3 cloves garlic, minced

¼ cup (30 g) all-purpose flour

1½ tsp (8 g) kosher salt, divided

4 cups (940 ml) reduced-sodium chicken stock

2 cups (470 ml) half-and-half

2 cups (140 g) roughly chopped broccoli florets

1½ tsp (3 g) freshly ground black pepper, divided

4 cups (480 g) freshly shredded sharp cheddar cheese

Melt the butter in a stockpot or 5½-quart (5-L) Dutch oven over medium-high heat. Add the onion and carrot. Cook until the onions are translucent, about 3 minutes. Add the garlic and cook for 30 seconds. Sprinkle the flour over the vegetables and stir until they are coated. Continue cooking for 3 minutes to cook out the floury taste, stirring occasionally.

Add 1 teaspoon of the salt, the chicken stock and half-and-half to the vegetables. Stir and bring to a simmer; cook until the soup has thickened, about 10 minutes. Add the broccoli and simmer until it is crisp-tender, about 5 minutes. Remove from the heat.

Add 1 teaspoon of the pepper and sprinkle the cheese into the soup a handful at a time. Stir until the cheese is melted before adding more cheese. Taste for seasoning. Add the remaining ½ teaspoon of salt and remaining ½ teaspoon of pepper if desired.

DONNA'S SIMPLE KITCHEN TIP: Reheat cheese soups and cheese sauces low and slow to maintain the smooth texture. Heating it too quickly can cause it to become grainy.

FIRE-ROASTED TOMATO BASIL SOUP

This tomato soup is rich and velvety with the concentrated flavor of basil shining though. It's utterly amazing, and naturally, it's perfect with grilled cheese. But, this ain't your mama's tomato soup. Fire-roasted tomatoes create that deep, long-cooked flavor without all the work, and aromatic Italian herbs add the perfect touch. The soup is finished with just enough cream to make it perfectly luscious without being heavy. The best part is, it freezes and reheats like a dream. I make a few batches and freeze it, so Chad can have this comforting soup whenever the mood strikes, and that happens quite often!

4 tbsp (56 g) unsalted butter

1 medium yellow onion, diced

4 cloves garlic, minced

¼ tsp crushed red pepper flakes

4 cups (940 ml) reduced-sodium chicken stock

1 (28-oz [784-g]) can crushed tomatoes

4 (14.5-oz [410-ml]) cans fire-roasted diced tomatoes

1 tbsp (5 g) dried basil

1 tbsp (3 g) Tuscan-Style Seasoning Blend (page 160)

1 tbsp (18 g) kosher salt

1 tbsp (6 g) freshly ground black pepper

½ cup (120 ml) heavy cream

In a stockpot over medium-high heat, melt the butter. Add the onions and cook until they begin to soften, about 3 minutes, stirring occasionally. Add the garlic and red pepper flakes and cook for 30 seconds.

Add the chicken stock, crushed and diced tomatoes, basil, seasoning blend, salt and pepper to the stockpot and stir to combine. Bring the soup to a boil and then reduce the heat to a simmer. Continue cooking, uncovered, for 15 minutes.

Carefully ladle the soup into a blender (be careful not to fill it more than half full) and puree. Then pour it back into the stockpot. Add the cream and stir to combine.

DONNA'S SIMPLE KITCHEN TIP: When freezing soups, allow the soup to cool before packing it up. Freeze it in small containers that are the size you will serve. We use 2- and 4-cup (470- and 940-ml) containers. Leave some room at the top of the container because the soup will expand as it freezes. Place a piece of plastic wrap over the top of the soup, under the lid, to help prevent freezer burn. When reheating, it is best to reheat low and slow due to the cream in the soup. If you are making it to freeze, leave out the cream and just add a splash when you reheat it.

CHICKEN ALFREDO TORTELLINI SOUP

Tender chunks of chicken, pasta and fresh veggies in a thick and creamy Parmesan cheese soup is utterly life changing! It's like your favorite Alfredo pasta transformed into a scrumptious bowl full of warm hugs. One bite is enough to make me do the happy dance. The soup all starts by building layers of flavor. Then you create an unbelievably rich Alfredo cream soup right on top of the sautéed vegetables and browned chicken. I add a pinch of red pepper flakes, because I love a little heat. And the pasta . . . I have a little bit of a tortellini thing. I guess you may have noticed. It's the perfect quick-cooking pasta, is amazing in everything and is stuffed with cheese. Yep, that was a no-brainer!

2 tbsp (28 g) unsalted butter

½ medium yellow onion, diced

4 oz (115 g) baby carrots, halved lengthwise and sliced into half-moons

2 cloves garlic, minced

1 lb (454 g) boneless skinless chicken breasts, cut into bite-size cubes

1 tsp kosher salt

½ tsp freshly ground black pepper

¼ cup (30 g) all-purpose flour

4 cups (940 ml) reduced-sodium chicken stock

1 cup (235 ml) half-and-half

1 tsp crushed red pepper flakes

9 oz (255 g) cheese tortellini, frozen or fresh

2 cups (200 g) freshly shredded Parmesan cheese

2 oz (56 g) fresh baby spinach

Warm a large pot over medium-high heat. Once you can feel the heat when you hold your hand 6 inches (15 cm) above the pot, add the butter and let it melt. Add the onion and carrots. Cook the vegetables until the onions are translucent, about 3 minutes. Add the garlic and cook for 30 seconds. Then add the chicken, salt and pepper. Stir to combine. Cook for 3 minutes, just to get a little color on the chicken, stirring occasionally. Don't worry about the chicken being cooked through, because we are going to continue cooking it.

Sprinkle the flour over the chicken and veggies. Stir to coat everything and continue cooking for 2 to 3 minutes to cook out the floury taste. Stir in the chicken stock, half-and-half and red pepper flakes. Continue cooking until the soup thickens, 5 to 10 minutes. Add the tortellini to the pot and cook until al dente (has a bite to it), 5 to 7 minutes (frozen takes longer). Remove the pot from the heat. Sprinkle a handful of cheese over the soup and stir. Once it has melted into the soup, add another handful. Slowly melting the cheese will give the soup a smooth consistency. Taste for seasoning and add salt and pepper as necessary. Pour into bowls and garnish with the spinach.

DONNA'S SIMPLE KITCHEN TIP: To reheat cream or cheese soup, warm it in a pot on the stove top over low heat, stirring frequently. Add milk to loosen the soup. Cheese- or milk-based soups need to be warmed slowly to prevent them from separating or having a grainy texture.

BUFFALO CHICKEN BEER CHEESE SOUP WITH RICE

When it comes to game day, nothing quite beats the taste of Buffalo wings, except when you combine those spicy and tangy flavors with a creamy beer cheese soup to get an all-time game-day hero in this completely satisfying "bowl of delicious" that will warm your soul. So, even when your team drops the ball, you can bring home a big win!

4 tbsp (56 g) unsalted butter

1 lb (454 g) boneless skinless chicken breasts, cut into bite-size pieces

½ tsp freshly cracked black pepper

½ tsp kosher salt

2 cups (470 ml) whole milk

1 cup (235 ml) beer or white ale

1 cup (235 ml) chicken stock

1 cup (190 g) uncooked long-grain jasmine rice

¼–½ cup (60–120 ml) Buffalo wings hot sauce, to taste

2 cups (240 g) freshly shredded pepper Jack cheese

1 cup (120 g) freshly shredded sharp cheddar cheese

Optional toppings: Blue cheese crumbles, croutons and chopped chives

Warm a 4-quart (3.6-L) saucepan over medium-high heat. Once you can feel the heat when you hold your hand 6 inches (15 cm) above the pot, add the butter. Season the chicken with the salt and pepper. Once the butter is melted, add the chicken pieces to the pot and cook, stirring occasionally, until the chicken is lightly browned. Don't worry if it isn't cooked through yet; we will be cooking it some more. Right now we are building flavor by getting that beautiful caramelization on the chicken.

Add the milk, beer, chicken stock, uncooked rice and hot sauce to the pot and stir to combine. Cover the pot and bring the soup to a boil. Then, reduce the heat to a simmer. Cook, covered, for 15 minutes, or until the rice is cooked.

Remove the cover and stir well, unsticking any rice that is on the bottom of the pot. Sprinkle the cheeses into the soup slowly as you stir, adding more and stirring after each addition until you have a smooth soup. If you add the cheese too quickly, it could cause the soup to become grainy.

Ladle into a bowl and top with blue cheese crumbles, croutons and chopped chives, if desired.

DONNA'S SIMPLE KITCHEN TIPS: Add hot sauce to taste: ¼ cup (60 ml) will yield a mild heat and ½ cup (120 ml) will yield a medium heat. If you are making the soup to serve later, make the rice separately and add it to the soup as you serve, so the rice doesn't absorb all of the liquid as it sits.

If you are sensitive to alcohol, you can substitute more chicken stock for the beer.

TUSCAN SAUSAGE POTATO SOUP

Sausage, potatoes and fresh kale in a perfectly seasoned rich and creamy broth made this Tuscan-inspired soup a hit from the first bite. I love the stick-to-your-ribs kind of soups. I mean, if I am going to have soup as a meal it needs to feel like a meal. So I upped the fixin's with big chunks of russet potatoes and lots of spicy Italian sausage. This is a meal that the whole family will love—restaurant-style in the comfort of your own home!

1 (1-lb [454-g]) package hot Italian sausage, casing removed

6 cups (1.4 L) reduced-sodium chicken stock

6 medium russet potatoes (2 lb [908 g]), cut into ½" (1.3-cm) cubes

½ tsp kosher salt, more to taste

½ tsp crushed red pepper flakes, more to taste

4 cups (280 g) chopped kale

1 cup (235 ml) heavy cream

Warm a Dutch oven or a 6-quart (5.4-L) pot over medium-high heat. Once you can feel the heat when you hold your hand 6 inches (15 cm) above the pot, crumble in the Italian sausage. Cook, stirring occasionally and breaking up the sausage as desired (I like bigger chunks), until the sausage is browned and cooked through, 5 to 7 minutes. Drain the sausage drippings from the pan.

Return the pot to the heat and add the chicken stock, potatoes, salt and red pepper flakes. Boil until the potatoes are fork-tender, about 15 minutes. Use a slotted spoon to remove 1 cup (180 g) of potatoes from the pot and place them in a bowl. Mash the potatoes and pour them back into the pot; this will help thicken the soup. Add the kale and cream to the soup, and stir to combine. Continue cooking the soup until the kale is wilted and tender, about 3 more minutes. Taste for seasoning and add salt to taste and red pepper flakes.

DONNA'S SIMPLE KITCHEN TIP: If you prefer, you can swap out the kale with baby spinach.

SIX

SIMPLE SIDES & VEGGIES

Putting together a fabulous dinner that you can be proud to feed your family is a matter of having great recipes at your fingertips. Sides that are easy to prepare are a really big part of that, and honestly, sometimes the side dishes are even better than the dinner—that is when you know it's good! Chad and I could literally eat these sides *as* the dinner; in fact, we actually have. If you are used to the standard steamed vegetables and a boiled potato as a side dish, then boy, are you in for a surprise.

Herb-Roasted Italian Vegetables (page 121) are so amazing it feels like cheating to actually call them vegetables. They are roasted until perfectly sweet and caramelized. Donna, party of one? Yep, winner, winner, vegetable dinner!

Restaurant-Style Mexican Rice (page 129) is a simple recipe that is great on its own or with chicken or steak stirred in. We also love it on burritos and I even eat it with my eggs in the morning. How versatile is that?

Garlic Roasted Bacon Brussels Sprouts (page 130) is the recipe you have been waiting for to turn you into a sprout lover. I have always been a "particular" eater, but I have decided that if I don't like it, it is just because it wasn't prepared right for me. So, I keep trying. Roasted Brussels are the perfect example. I absolutely love them now and can eat a whole pan by myself!

Mexican Tortellini Salad with Chile-Lime Dressing (page 133) is one of my favorite pasta salads ever. It's loaded with some of my beloved Mexican flavors and is a crowd-pleaser. Naturally, it is perfect as a side, but I love the leftovers for lunch. When I put this one on the potluck table, it disappears like magic!

Garlic-Parmesan Smashed Potatoes (page 126) are Chad's most requested side dish. He even picks up the ingredients at the store and sneaks them into the cart when I'm not looking. True story. I love when a recipe is *that* inspiring.

Pick a side, and satisfy the craving!

HERB-ROASTED ITALIAN VEGETABLES

These splendidly seasoned, sweet caramelized vegetables taste like candy and are so easy to make. Zucchini, eggplant, baby red potatoes and carrots are tossed in a blend of Italian seasoning with tomatoes, onions and garlic and roasted to perfection! When you need to take dinner to the next level, simply add a pan of these Herb-Roasted Italian Vegetables to the menu. That's taking dinnertime to WOW time. Just toss, season and bake. Holy yum!

1 medium zucchini

½ medium eggplant

1 lb (454 g) baby red potatoes

1 cup (150 g) grape tomatoes

1 cup (120 g) baby carrots

1 medium red onion

2 tbsp (6 g) Tuscan-Style Seasoning Blend (page 160)

1 tsp kosher salt

¼ cup (60 ml) extra virgin olive oil

Preheat the oven to 400°F (200°C, or gas mark 6). Line a sheet pan with foil and set aside.

Cut the veggies into ½-inch (1.3-cm) bite-size pieces and spread them on the sheet pan. Sprinkle the vegetables with the seasoning and salt, then drizzle with the olive oil and toss with clean hands.

Roast for 30 to 40 minutes, stirring the vegetables every 15 minutes, until the carrots and potatoes are fork-tender and the vegetables start to brown around the edges. Taste for seasoning, and add extra salt as desired.

DONNA'S SIMPLE KITCHEN TIP: To save time on busy weeknights, I prep the vegetables the night before, add them to a gallon-size (3.6-L) zip-top bag and store in the refrigerator until the next day. While you are preheating the oven, add the seasoning, salt and oil to the bag. Seal and shake to combine. Then pour everything onto a foil-lined sheet pan and bake.

BEST EVER SLOW COOKER CREAMED CORN

This slow cooker creamed corn is silky, sweet and totally delicious. The recipe is so easy—simply toss seven ingredients into the slow cooker and a few hours later it's done. Sweet corn in a rich and creamy sauce makes this an impressive go-to holiday side, but we love it any night of the week. Every time I make this creamed corn my daughter Sierra tells me, "Mommy, aren't we supposed to have dinner before dessert?" It's just that good!

8 oz (227 g) cream cheese, cut into pieces

1 cup (235 ml) whole milk

½ cup (120 ml) heavy cream

4 tbsp (56 g) unsalted butter

3 tbsp (36 g) sugar

1 tsp kosher salt

2 lb (908 g) frozen corn

Freshly ground black pepper, to taste

Combine the cream cheese, milk, cream, butter, sugar, salt and corn in the slow cooker; I use a 5-quart (4.5-L) round for this. Stir everything together as best you can. Cover and cook on low for 4 hours, stirring occasionally. At about 3 hours it will come together, but it won't be completely thickened. Allow it to cook for the full 4 hours for the best results. Season with black pepper to taste.

DONNA'S SIMPLE KITCHEN TIP: The sauce will thicken as it sits, so you may wish to add a little milk if you would like it to stay in the slow cooker longer. I make this Thanksgiving morning, and when it is done, I turn it to the warm setting and stir it from time to time, adding just a little more milk when it gets too thick.

SERVES 6

10-MINUTE GARLIC-PARMESAN BROCCOLI

Crisp-tender broccoli with garlic is topped with nutty Parmesan cheese and just a pinch of red pepper flakes to make this recipe one of the many reasons Sierra and I are big-time broccoli lovers through and through! When I was a kid, I would hide my broccoli so I didn't have to eat it. Now you have to hide it from me so I don't eat it all. Funny how things change!

2 tbsp (28 g) unsalted butter

4 cloves garlic, thinly sliced

¼ tsp crushed red pepper flakes

¼ cup (60 ml) water

1 lb (454 g) broccoli florets, cut into 1" (2.5-cm) pieces

½ cup (50 g) freshly shredded Parmesan cheese

½ tsp kosher salt

Melt the butter in a large skillet over medium-high heat, and then add the garlic and red pepper flakes. Cook until the garlic is golden and fragrant, about 1 minute, stirring occasionally.

Add the water and broccoli florets to the pan and bring the water to a boil. Cover and cook until the broccoli is crisp-tender, about 3 minutes. Remove the cover and simmer until most of the liquid has evaporated, about 1 minute. Sprinkle the broccoli with the Parmesan cheese and salt. Stir to combine.

DONNA'S SIMPLE KITCHEN TIP: Save time and buy broccoli florets already trimmed in the produce section.

GARLIC-PARMESAN SMASHED POTATOES

Tender garlic herb potatoes are smashed and roasted with nutty Parmesan cheese until perfectly crisp and delicious to create this absolutely divine dish! These potatoes are absolutely divine! Truth be told, Chad and I ate these as a game-day treat several weekends in a row: We piled them high and ate 'em like French fries. Just one bite and you will never make plain boring potatoes again.

2 lb (908 g) baby potatoes

4 tsp (24 g) kosher salt, divided

8 tbsp (112 g) unsalted butter

6 cloves garlic, roughly chopped

2 tbsp (3 g) chopped fresh rosemary

½ tsp freshly ground black pepper

½ cup (50 g) freshly shredded Parmesan cheese

Chopped fresh Italian parsley, for garnish

Preheat the oven to 425°F (220°C, or gas mark 7). Line a baking sheet with aluminum foil, for easy cleanup.

Place the potatoes in a heavy-bottomed pot over high heat. Add enough water to cover the tops of the potatoes. Add 3 teaspoons (18 g) of the salt to the water. Cover and boil the potatoes until they are fork-tender, about 15 minutes.

Meanwhile, in a small bowl, combine the butter, garlic, rosemary, remaining 1 teaspoon of salt and the pepper. Mix well. Microwave the mixture until the butter is melted and warm; this will help infuse the garlic and rosemary into the butter. Stir and set aside.

Use a slotted spoon to scoop the potatoes out of the pot and onto the prepared baking sheet. Pour the herb butter mixture over the potatoes. Toss with a spoon to coat. Use the flat bottom of a glass or measuring cup to smash the potatoes to about ½-inch (1.3-cm) thick.

Flip the smashed potatoes over so both sides are well coated in the herbs and butter. Sprinkle the potatoes with the shredded cheese. Bake for 20 minutes, or until the cheese is melted and the bottoms of the potatoes have begun to brown. Sprinkle with the fresh parsley.

DONNA'S SIMPLE KITCHEN TIP: To help potatoes last for months, store them in a cool (less than 50°F [10°C] is optimum), dark, dry place. Do not store in a plastic bag. A well-ventilated mesh bag, flat bin or paper bag is a much better option. Keep away from onions; they will cause each other to spoil faster.

RESTAURANT-STYLE MEXICAN RICE

This restaurant-inspired Mexican rice is exploding with smoky flavors, a rich tomato base and just the right amount of jalapeños, tomatoes and corn. We love Mexican food, and quite often when we dine out it is at a Mexican restaurant. The rice is always so amazing, so we had to create our own version to enjoy at home! The whole family goes crazy over this recipe. I eat it right out of the pan—you have to taste test, right? But I was busted when they walked in while I was happy dancing over the pan. Honestly, I would be fine with eating this as my entire dinner, but the responsible adult in me kicks in . . . well, at least when my daughter is around.

3 tbsp (45 ml) extra virgin olive oil

½ medium white onion, diced

1–3 jalapeño peppers, seeded and minced

3 cloves garlic, minced

2 cups (380 g) long-grain jasmine rice

2 cups (470 ml) chicken stock

1 (14.5-oz [410-ml]) can fire-roasted diced tomatoes

8 oz (227 g) tomato sauce

1 cup (130 g) corn (frozen, fresh or canned and drained)

2 tbsp (14 g) Mexican Seasoning Blend (page 160)

1 tsp kosher salt

Chopped fresh cilantro

Warm the oil in a 10-inch (25.4-cm) skillet over medium heat. Once you can feel the heat when you hold your hand 6 inches (15 cm) above the skillet, add the onion and jalapeños to the pan and cook until the onions begin to soften, 2 to 3 minutes, stirring occasionally. Add the garlic and stir. Continue cooking for 30 seconds.

Add the rice and stir until it is well coated in the oil. Cook until the rice starts to brown, 3 to 4 minutes, stirring occasionally. Add the chicken stock, tomatoes, tomato sauce, corn, seasoning blend and salt. Stir to combine and bring to a boil.

Cover the pot, decrease the heat to a simmer and cook until the rice is cooked through, 12 to 15 minutes. Remove from the heat and sprinkle with the cilantro.

DONNA'S SIMPLE KITCHEN TIP: Customize your heat level. Add one jalapeño for mild, two for medium and three for hot.

GARLIC ROASTED BACON BRUSSELS SPROUTS

Caramelized oven-roasted Brussels sprouts transformed me into a sprout lover! They are slightly crisp on the outside and tender on the inside. I have never liked sprouts, until now. The addition of bacon and red pepper flakes really takes these sprouts over the top. Honestly, I can't get enough. The first time I made them, I ate the entire pan. Yes, all by myself. Quick! Someone hide the sprouts!

2 lb (908 g) fresh Brussels sprouts, cut in half lengthwise (top to bottom)

1 medium red onion, roughly chopped

6 cloves garlic, roughly chopped

1 tsp kosher salt

1 tsp freshly ground black pepper

Pinch of crushed red pepper flakes

2 tbsp (30 ml) extra virgin olive oil

8 slices uncooked thick-cut bacon, cut into ½" (1.3-cm) strips

Preheat the oven to 425°F (220°C, or gas mark 7). Line a sheet pan with aluminum foil.

Spread the Brussels sprouts, onions and garlic on the pan. Sprinkle the sprouts with the salt, pepper and red pepper flakes, then drizzle with the olive oil. Toss the sprouts with clean hands until everything is well coated.

Wiggle the pan until the Brussels sprouts are in a single layer. Sprinkle the cut bacon pieces over the pan evenly. Bake for 20 to 25 minutes, until the sprouts are fork-tender. Taste and season with additional salt if necessary.

DONNA'S SIMPLE KITCHEN TIP: Kitchen shears are an awesome kitchen tool. The easiest way to cut bacon is to stack two or three slices on top of one another and cut them with kitchen shears. Kitchen shears are also great for snipping and chopping herbs, opening packages and cutting chicken. The possibilities are endless, but cutting bacon is my favorite way to use them.

MEXICAN TORTELLINI SALAD WITH CHILE-LIME DRESSING

This glorious salad is loaded with fresh veggies, tortellini pasta and incredible Mexican flavors. The chile-lime dressing is a little smoky, spicy and tart. Poured over fresh veggies, black beans, pasta and cheese, it is purely crave-worthy. I could live on this salad; I mean, Mexican flavors and tortellini pasta—what's not to love?

DRESSING

¼ cup (60 ml) extra light olive oil

2 tbsp (28 g) mayonnaise

¼ cup (60 ml) fresh lime juice

1 tbsp (6 g) lime zest

2 tbsp (40 g) honey

2 tbsp (30 g) tomato paste

1 tsp New Mexico chile powder

½ tsp crushed red pepper flakes

½ tsp kosher salt

2 cloves garlic, grated on a microplane or finely minced

SALAD

1 (19-oz [532-g]) package cheese tortellini

1 lb (454 g) grape tomatoes, halved

¼ red onion, thinly sliced

1 orange bell pepper, cored, seeded and cut into bite-size pieces

1 English cucumber, cut into spears and then quartered

1 (15.25-oz [430-g]) can corn, rinsed and drained

1 (15-oz [425-ml]) can reduced-sodium black beans, rinsed and drained

4 oz (112 g) Colby Jack cheese, cut into bite-size cubes

To make the dressing, in a large bowl, combine all of the dressing ingredients. Whisk until well blended. Set aside.

To make the salad, bring a large pot of salted water to a boil over medium-high heat. Cook the tortellini according to the package directions. Drain the pasta, add to the dressing and toss to combine. The hot tortellini will soak up some of the dressing and give it an amazing flavor.

Add the tomatoes, onion, bell pepper, cucumber, corn and beans to the bowl and toss to combine with the tortellini and dressing. Top with the cheese.

DONNA'S SIMPLE KITCHEN TIP: In the summer, use corn kernels sliced off grilled corn on the cob in place of the canned corn kernels. It adds an amazing layer of flavor.

SPICED BROWN SUGAR ROASTED SWEET POTATOES

Here, golden, caramelized, roasted sweet potatoes are perfectly tender with a scrumptious flavor combination of brown sugar, cinnamon and cayenne pepper to create a flavor explosion. We all love sweet potato casserole for Thanksgiving, but for an out-of-this-world recipe that you would be happy to devour all year long . . . this is it! Chad and I love these so much we eat them right off the baking pan. When that oven timer goes off, we are already at the stove, forks in hand.

4 tbsp (56 g) unsalted butter, melted

2 tbsp (25 g) packed light brown sugar

½ tsp ground cinnamon

½ tsp kosher salt

¼ tsp cayenne pepper

2 large sweet potatoes, peeled and cut into ½" (1.3-cm) cubes

Preheat the oven to 450°F (230°C, or gas mark 8). Line a baking sheet with aluminum foil.

Melt the butter in a small microwave-safe bowl. Add the brown sugar, cinnamon, salt and cayenne pepper to the bowl and stir to combine.

Spread the sweet potatoes on the baking sheet. Pour the brown sugar mixture over them and toss with clean hands until the potatoes are completely coated. Bake for 20 to 25 minutes, stirring once halfway through.

DONNA'S SIMPLE KITCHEN TIP: Large sweet potatoes can be challenging to cut. Try using a sharp chef's knife and a cutting board with a damp paper towel underneath (to help keep it from sliding). Slice the sweet potato in half lengthwise and then lay the halves, cut side down, on your board. Cut into slices again. If your potato is too thick, you can flip your slices over and cut them in half. Then cut the slices into cubes.

CHEESY ITALIAN HERB ORZO

Rice-shaped pasta, called orzo, is toasted in butter and then topped in a divinely rich and creamy Parmesan cheese sauce with fresh herbs sprinkled in to add amazing Italian flavor. Leftovers? Nope. Luckily, this simple recipe is an amazing stove-top side dish that comes together quickly, so I can make it again and again. It is truly the ultimate pasta side!

2 tbsp (28 g) unsalted butter

1 shallot, minced

2 cloves garlic, minced

1 cup (160 g) orzo pasta, uncooked (not the whole box)

2 cups (470 ml) reduced-sodium chicken stock

1 cup (235 ml) half-and-half

½ cup (50 g) freshly grated Parmesan cheese

1 tbsp (3 g) chopped fresh basil

1 tbsp (2 g) chopped fresh rosemary

1 tbsp (4 g) chopped fresh Italian parsley

Salt and pepper to taste

Melt the butter in a 10-inch (25.4-cm) skillet over medium-high heat. Add the shallot and cook until it becomes translucent, about 2 minutes. Then add the garlic and cook for 30 seconds.

Add the orzo to the skillet. Cook until the orzo is lightly toasted and golden brown, 2 to 3 minutes, stirring occasionally. Add the chicken stock and half-and-half. Stir, cover and bring to a boil. Decrease the heat to a simmer and cook until the liquid is mostly absorbed, 8 to 9 minutes.

Sprinkle the cheese over the pasta and stir until the cheese is melted. Add the fresh herbs and stir to combine. Season with salt and pepper to taste.

DONNA'S SIMPLE KITCHEN TIP: Fresh herbs like parsley and cilantro will keep for weeks in the fridge. Remove the herbs from the grocery store produce bag and set the bag aside. Fill a mason jar with 1 inch (2.5 cm) of water. Trim the ends off of the herbs and also remove the wilted leaves. Place the herbs in the water and cover loosely with the plastic bag. Place in the refrigerator. Use as desired. Refill the water as needed. I have kept my herbs fresh for 2 to 3 weeks this way.

HONEY-GINGER GLAZED CARROTS

Baby carrots are cooked to perfection in a sweet orange and honey-ginger glaze. The ginger really revs up the flavor and helps balance out the sweetness. Chad is a huge carrot lover, so much so that I used to make him a big bag of sweet steamed carrots each week. Yes, seriously! These are so much better! Honey-Ginger Glazed Carrots are a super simple crowd-pleasing veggie dish. Bye-bye, boring steamed carrots!

¼ cup (60 ml) orange juice

¼ cup (80 g) honey

4 tbsp (56 g) unsalted butter

1 tbsp (6 g) freshly minced ginger (or ginger paste)

1½ tsp (9 g) kosher salt

1 lb (454 g) baby carrots

Small handful of fresh Italian parsley, chopped

Combine the orange juice, honey, butter, ginger and salt in a 10-inch (25.4-cm) skillet over medium heat. Stir to combine. Add the carrots and toss until they are coated. Cover the skillet and bring to a boil. Cook the carrots until they are almost tender (when a fork will just pierce the carrot, but it is not yet tender), 6 to 8 minutes.

Remove the cover and continue to cook until the liquid becomes thick like a syrup and coats the back of a spoon, 4 to 5 minutes. Garnish with the fresh parsley.

DONNA'S SIMPLE KITCHEN TIP: Lightly spray the inside of your measuring cup with nonstick cooking spray before measuring the honey. It will slide out easily and not stick to the cup.

SEVEN

EVERYDAY KITCHEN ESSENTIALS

Since we started our website, The Slow Roasted Italian, we have created more than 1,000 recipes. So, as you can imagine, we enjoy a lot of new creations. There are some recipes that have become staples in our kitchen. We have found that they are absolutely essential to having a simple kitchen, and they include everything from our go-to seasoning blends to gravy and sauces that we use quite often to create quick and easy dinners when we haven't planned ahead. After all, the true key to a simple kitchen is having your toolbox filled with scrumptious, foolproof recipes.

The Everything Cheese Sauce (page 144) has to be my favorite recipe in this chapter. It is the perfect consistency and has amazing flavor. I drizzle it over everything—I have even poured it over a pound (454 g) of cooked pasta for a yummy and quick mac and cheese. I mean, let's be honest here: It's a dynamite pepper Jack cheese sauce, and I would live on cheese if I could. Wait . . . can I? I can't even count how many times I have made it, but believe me, it is a game changer. Happy dance? I downright got my dancing shoes on after this one!

I know it's hard to follow up the cheese sauce of the century, but if there were a recipe that could give it a run for its money, it would be the Italian Herb Baked Meatballs (page 143). I have been making these baked meatballs for years and they are still our favorite. I am a bit of a meatball snob—even from a young age I was critiquing meatballs at family gatherings—so you better believe these tender and juicy meatballs are bursting with fresh herbs and beefy flavor.

Our No-Rise Pizza Dough (page 159) is perfect for stromboli, calzones, bread sticks and, of course, pizza. It comes together in 15 minutes and then it's ready to be topped with whatever you like. Our 5-Ingredient Alfredo Sauce (page 155), 10-Minute Marinara Arrabbiata (page 147) or Perfect Basil Pesto (page 156) would be a great place to start.

There are so many amazing recipes in this chapter. We have had them all in a binder right next to our stove for a long, long time, and we are thrilled to share them with you. Enjoy the essentials—they are going to change your life!

ITALIAN HERB BAKED MEATBALLS

These are truly the most amazing meatballs we have ever had. They are beautifully browned on the outside and tender and juicy on the inside. What's more, they are baked, not fried, and bursting with Italian flavors. They're perfectly cheesy and utterly addictive. We make several batches of meatballs at a time and eat them right off the tray, no sauce required. One for you, two for me. These are the best dang meatballs ever!

1 lb (454 g) lean ground beef (I used 85% lean)

½ cup (30 g) Italian seasoned breadcrumbs

¼ cup (25 g) freshly grated Parmesan cheese

½ small onion, diced

2 tbsp (30 ml) milk

1 tbsp (2 g) chopped fresh rosemary

1 tbsp (4 g) chopped fresh Italian parsley

1 tbsp (3 g) chopped fresh basil

1½ tsp (9 g) kosher salt

½ tsp freshly cracked black pepper

2 cloves garlic, minced

1 large egg, lightly beaten

Olive oil, for hands

Preheat the oven to 375°F (190°C, or gas mark 5). Line a baking sheet with parchment paper and set aside.

In a large mixing bowl, combine the beef, breadcrumbs, cheese, onion, milk, herbs, salt, pepper, garlic and egg and use clean hands to gently mix everything until well-blended. Be careful not to overmix or your meatballs will be tough, and tough meatballs are *no bueno!*

Using a 2-tablespoon (28-g) scoop (or a 1-tablespoon [14-g] scoop for appetizer- and soup-size meatballs), portion out the meatballs and place them on the prepared baking sheet. After you scoop the meatballs onto the baking sheet, lightly oil your hands with olive oil to prevent the meatballs from sticking to you and roll them into balls.

Bake for 20 to 22 minutes, until the meatballs are browned and cooked through. You can transfer them to your sauce or enjoy them straight from the pan, like I said, no sauce required!

DONNA'S SIMPLE KITCHEN TIPS: Use a scoop to make uniform-size meatballs; this way, you handle them less and they will cook evenly. Make these ahead and freeze them for quick dinners.

For an even more flavorful meatball, you can substitute whatever sauce you are serving in place of the milk.

ESSENTIAL IN: Meatball Parmesan Skillet (page 46), French Onion Meatball Soup (page 104) and Slow Cooker Bourbon Brown Sugar Meatballs (page 85)

MAKES 1½ CUPS (355 ML)

EVERYTHING CHEESE SAUCE

Everything Cheese Sauce is the most amazing pepper Jack–cheddar cheese sauce that you will ever eat. It truly is everything! Inspired by our Triple Cheesy Mac and Cheese (page 14), it is a rock star in the kitchen. It is rich and creamy with the perfect little kick, and it comes together in 10 minutes. I love to add a spoonful to Sierra's veggies. Chad and I gobble it up by the bucketful with nachos. It calls to me from the refrigerator at night. So, what's a girl to do? I can officially say this cheese sauce tastes great on everything . . . including a spoon, just saying.

2 tbsp (28 g) unsalted butter

2 tbsp (16 g) all-purpose flour

½ tsp kosher salt

½ tsp cayenne pepper

1½ cups (355 ml) whole milk

½ cup (60 g) freshly shredded pepper Jack cheese

½ cup (60 g) freshly shredded sharp cheddar cheese

8 oz (227 g) Velveeta cheese, cut into chunks

In a small saucepan over medium heat, melt the butter. Add the flour, salt and cayenne pepper and whisk to combine. Cook for 1 minute to cook out the floury taste. Don't skip this step. Trust me, floury sauce is not tasty, and cooking it for a minute will also brown the flour, adding a slight nuttiness to your cheese sauce.

Add the milk, whisking constantly. Simmer until the sauce begins to steam, about 3 minutes. Decrease the heat to low. Add the cheeses a handful at a time, whisking after each addition until the cheese melts into the sauce. Lift your whisk out of the sauce. If there are still cheese shreds on the whisk, keep stirring. Continue adding the cheese and whisking until all the cheese is melted into the sauce, and then stir the sauce until it's well-combined.

The sauce will keep in the refrigerator in a mason jar for 3 to 4 days.

DONNA'S SIMPLE KITCHEN TIP: When making cheese sauces and cheese-based soups, be sure to add the cheese slowly over low heat, or your sauce could become grainy. Reheat cheese sauces and soups low and slow to maintain the smooth texture.

ESSENTIAL IN: Stacked Cantina Nachos (page 86)

READY IN 10 MIN

**MAKES
1 (24-OZ
[705-ML]) JAR**

10-MINUTE MARINARA ARRABBIATA

Our favorite spicy marinara comes together in just 10 minutes and has a rich tomato flavor with just enough heat to make your taste buds stand up and dance. It is our go-to red gravy (as my dad calls it) and is perfect over pasta and meatballs, on pizza and as a dipping sauce. I have always made my all-day tomato sauce for the holidays, but truth be told, I have been making this simple marinara sauce for several Christmas dinners now, and everyone absolutely goes crazy over it! No one can tell the difference. (*Shhhh!*) I won't tell if you don't.

1 (14.5-oz [410-ml]) can fire-roasted diced tomatoes

1 (15-oz [425-ml]) can tomato sauce

1 tbsp (3 g) Tuscan-Style Seasoning Blend (page 160)

1 tbsp (12 g) sugar

1 tsp garlic powder

1 tsp onion powder

1 tsp kosher salt

½–1 tsp crushed red pepper flakes, to taste

½ tsp freshly ground black pepper

Combine all of the ingredients in a medium saucepan over medium-high heat and stir until the sauce is well-mixed. Decrease the heat to a simmer and cook for 5 minutes, or keep warm on low heat until you are ready to serve. If you prefer your sauce smooth, you can puree it in the pot with an immersion blender or add all of the ingredients to a countertop blender, puree and then transfer to the saucepan to cook.

DONNA'S SIMPLE KITCHEN TIPS: Adding sugar to tomato-based recipes helps balance the tartness and coax the sweet side out of the tomatoes.

Add the red pepper flakes according to your desired heat level. We like it about medium spicy, so 1 teaspoon is perfect. If you have no tolerance for heat, just leave it out and you will have a fabulous marinara.

ESSENTIAL IN: Garlic-Parmesan Pizza Pinwheels (page 78), Meatball Parmesan Skillet (page 46), Three-Cheese Meat Lasagna (page 10) and Crunchy Baked Chicken Strips (page 68)

40-MINUTE MILK AND HONEY DINNER ROLLS

This bread is slightly sweet with a buttery crust. We transformed our go-to milk and honey sliced bread into these fabulous dinner rolls that come together with no rise time. Seriously, no rise time! When they come out of the oven, we usually finish off almost half a pan while the rolls are hot and fresh. These rolls are so magical that I made them for Thanksgiving this year. Everyone loved them and ate them all. Every last one! So, the moral of the story is: If you want leftovers, be sure to tuck them away before you serve them or there won't be any left.

5 tbsp (70 g) unsalted butter, melted, divided

4½ tsp (18 g) active dry yeast (2 packets)

1¼ cups (295 ml) warm milk (110°–115°F [43°–46°C])

¼ cup (80 g) honey

3½–4 cups (420–480 g) all-purpose flour, divided

1½ tsp (9 g) kosher salt

DONNA'S SIMPLE KITCHEN TIP: To hand mix, add the yeast, warm milk and honey to a large bowl. Once the yeast blooms, about 3 minutes, stir in 3 tablespoons of (42 g) butter, flour and salt. Mix with a spoon until you cannot mix the dough any longer, then turn the dough out onto the floured countertop and knead for 3 to 5 minutes, until the dough is slightly sticky. Proceed with the instructions.

ESSENTIAL IN: Overnight Cinnamon Rolls (page 181), Hot Ham and Cheese Party Sliders (page 94) and Crazy Caramel Apple Pie Bombs (page 182)

Preheat the oven to 350°F (180°C, or gas mark 4). Grease a 9 x 13-inch (23 x 33-cm) baking pan with 1 tablespoon (14 g) of the melted butter and set it on the stove top to keep it slightly warm.

In the bowl of a stand mixer fitted with a dough hook, combine the yeast, warm milk and honey. Swirl the mixture with a spoon to dissolve the yeast. Let the mixture rest until the yeast becomes foamy and aromatic, about 3 minutes.

Add 3 tablespoons (42 g) of the butter and 3½ cups (420 g) of the flour to the stand mixer and mix on low until smooth. Add enough of the remaining ½ cup (60 g) of flour to form a soft dough (mine takes ¼–½ cup [30–60 g] more). Add the salt and knead on medium to medium-high speed for about 3 minutes. You should have a ball of slightly sticky dough at this point. When you press your fingertip into the dough and pull it away, some of the dough will stick to you. It is important to leave the dough sticky for the recipe; it aids in giving the bread some lift.

Turn the dough out onto a lightly floured countertop and form it into a ball. Divide the dough into 12 pieces and form them into balls by flipping the dough over and pulling the edges together to the bottom. Then place the dough balls, pinched side down, in the baking pan.

Bake for 15 to 17 minutes, or until golden brown. If the tops begin to brown too quickly, lightly tent the rolls with foil for the remainder of the cooking time. Remove the rolls from the oven and brush the tops with the remaining 1 tablespoon (14 g) of melted butter.

To make these overnight, prepare the recipe as written. Once you place the rolls in the pan, cover with plastic wrap and pop them in the refrigerator. The next morning, remove the plastic, preheat the oven and bake them for 17 to 20 minutes, until golden brown and cooked through.

RESTAURANT-STYLE CHUNKY SALSA

We finally have the restaurant secrets to the best salsa ever! We have devoured our share of chips and salsa at our favorite Mexican restaurants and trust me, we have had your share too. All in the name of research, of course. Ahem. And after many bowls, tons of questions and recipe testing, we have the ultimate salsa that tastes like your favorite Mexican restaurant. It's the perfect medium-heat salsa with chunks of roasted tomato, bits of onion, jalapeño and garlic. It has a brightness from lime juice and a little smokiness from cumin, with just the right kick of spice. We have been making this recipe for years, and everyone we know loves it. We just can't get enough. It is the perfect consistency for chips and is completely addictive. I mean, it's pretty much a meal on its own!

¼ medium white onion

1 medium jalapeño pepper, stemmed and halved

2 cloves garlic

1 (14.5-oz [410-ml]) can fire-roasted diced tomatoes

1 tbsp (15 ml) fresh lime juice (about ½ lime)

½ tsp kosher salt

¼ tsp sugar

¼ tsp ground cumin

2 tbsp (2 g) chopped fresh cilantro

Add the onion, jalapeño and garlic to the bowl of a food processor and pulse until you reach your desired consistency, 5 or 6 pulses. Open the cover and scrape down the sides of the bowl. Add the tomatoes, lime juice, salt, sugar, cumin and cilantro and pulse 1 or 2 times to combine. (You can also do this in a blender.)

Transfer the salsa to a serving dish and serve immediately, or transfer to a pint-size (470-ml) jar and store in the refrigerator. It becomes even more flavorful the next day. The salsa will keep fresh in the refrigerator for 3 to 4 days.

CHOOSE YOUR HEAT PREFERENCE:
Mild salsa: Remove the veins and seeds from the jalapeño.
Medium salsa: Prepare as written.
Hot salsa: Use 2 jalapeños, veins and seeds included.

DONNA'S SIMPLE KITCHEN TIP: Fire-roasted diced tomatoes are the real secret to making this restaurant-quality salsa at home. Try using them in quick-fix dinners for a hint of that long-cooked roasted flavor that we all know and love. It's one of my favorite simple kitchen tricks.

ESSENTIAL IN: Stacked Cantina Nachos (page 86) and Fiesta Chicken Street Tacos (page 18)

**MAKES
2 CUPS
(470 ML)**

5-MINUTE FOOLPROOF PERFECT HERB GRAVY

This perfect gravy is rich and creamy and totally herbaceous! It is completely bursting with flavor, insanely delicious and the only gravy recipe you will ever need. The dried herbs add a rich depth of flavor that taste like you spent a long time cooking. It is absolutely glorious and one of our favorite kitchen staples. Gravy was a necessity in my mom's kitchen when I was growing up. It seemed to be the beginning or the end to so many favorite recipes, and she could always make a meal around it. Of course, I married a meat-and-potatoes lover, so naturally gravy is an essential in our kitchen now, too. One day I caught Chad ladling out a bowl of gravy . . . for his dinner. Yep. True story, folks. We are a match made in gravy heaven!

2 cups (470 ml) reduced-sodium beef or chicken stock

2 beef or chicken bouillon cubes

4 tbsp (56 g) unsalted butter

¼ cup (30 g) all-purpose flour

1 tsp onion powder

¼ tsp dried thyme

½ tsp dried sage

1 tsp dried rosemary

Salt and pepper, to taste

Combine the stock and the bouillon cubes in a microwave-safe container (use all chicken for chicken gravy or all beef for beef gravy). I use my 2-cup (470-ml) glass, microwave-safe measuring cup. Heat for 1 minute and stir. Repeat until the bouillon cubes have dissolved, about 2 minutes.

Melt the butter in a medium saucepan over medium-high heat. Add the flour, onion powder, thyme, sage and rosemary. Whisk to combine and cook for 1 minute, whisking occasionally to cook out the floury taste. Add the hot stock to the flour mixture and whisk. Bring the gravy to a boil, decrease the heat to a simmer and whisk until it is as smooth as silk, about 1 minute. Taste and season with salt and pepper as desired. I add about ½ teaspoon of pepper.

DONNA'S SIMPLE KITCHEN TIP: Using unsalted butter allows you to control how much salt goes into your recipes, not to mention it is slightly sweeter and fresher. Salt is a preservative, so salted butter has a longer shelf life. So, naturally, unsalted butter is fresher. If you do not have unsalted butter, you can substitute with regular salted butter and decrease the salt called for in a recipe by half. Then add salt as needed.

ESSENTIAL IN: This gravy is the ultimate meal starter. It's perfect over cooked beef, potatoes, chicken and so much more.

**MAKES
1½ CUPS
(355 ML)**

5-INGREDIENT ALFREDO SAUCE

Alfredo is a classic Italian-American cheese sauce that is utterly rich and creamy. The addition of nutmeg lends warmth and elevates the flavor; it tastes like heaven on a spoon. This recipe comes together in just 15 minutes, which is so much faster than the wait time at your favorite Italian restaurant. It is so easy to pour over pasta. Add veggies and chicken or shrimp and you have dinner in just a few minutes! Yes, I admit it. I love, love, love this cheese sauce, and after you try this, so will you!

6 tbsp (84 g) unsalted butter

1 cup (235 ml) half-and-half

2 cloves garlic, minced

2 cups (200 g) freshly grated Parmesan cheese

Pinch of freshly grated nutmeg

Salt and pepper, to taste

In a medium saucepan over medium heat, melt the butter. Add the half-and-half to the melted butter while whisking. Add the garlic and simmer for 3 minutes. Make sure the cream mixture does not come to a boil.

Remove the sauce from the heat and add the cheese a handful at a time, whisking thoroughly until it is completely melted into the sauce, and then add the next handful and repeat until all the cheese has been added to the sauce. Add the nutmeg and stir. Taste the sauce, and add salt and pepper if needed.

DONNA'S SIMPLE KITCHEN TIP: Adding nutmeg to white sauces and meat recipes will give it that "oh my word, what's in this?" effect! Just a pinch of freshly ground nutmeg adds a mysterious flavor that enhances the recipe but isn't overwhelming.

OPTIONAL IN: Garlic-Parmesan Pizza Pinwheels (page 78)

MAKES 1 HEAPING CUP (260 G)

PERFECT BASIL PESTO

Nothing is quite as summery and fresh as homemade pesto, and it's great on just about everything. This recipe is perfectly bright, nutty, cheesy and oh so yummy! Planting an herb garden is one of my favorite things to do in the spring. Chad built the most beautiful garden boxes for us to plant, so Sierra and I geek out together planning what to grow in the garden. We always have so many basil plants, and what else is there to do with all that delicious basil but turn it into a scrumptious pesto? Honestly, Chad never really liked pesto until I started making it from fresh basil. Now he devours my pesto pasta sauce. And I love it so much that I may even sneak a spoonful from time to time, but that can be our little secret.

¼ cup (35 g) pine nuts, toasted (See tip on page 71 for toasting nuts)

2 cups (80 g) packed fresh basil leaves

2 cloves garlic

½ cup (50 g) freshly shredded Parmesan cheese

¾–1 tsp kosher salt, divided

½ cup (120 ml) extra virgin olive oil, plus extra for storing

In the bowl of a food processor or a blender, combine the pine nuts, basil, garlic, cheese and ½ teaspoon of the salt. Pulse until a smooth paste forms, about 2 minutes. Scrape down the sides of the bowl with a spatula and then replace the lid. Slowly drizzle the olive oil through the feed tube with the food processor running. Once the pesto comes together, taste for seasoning. Add more salt as desired. Mine takes ¼ to ½ teaspoon more, depending on the cheese I use.

Pour the pesto into an airtight container, pour a little olive oil on top and then press plastic wrap over the pesto to keep it fresh and green. Refrigerate until ready to serve. Store the pesto in the refrigerator for up to 1 week or freeze for 3 months.

DONNA'S SIMPLE KITCHEN TIP: I know summer doesn't last forever, but your pesto can. Well, at least for several months. Freeze the pesto in ice cube trays and then transfer to a zip-top freezer bag to store in the freezer. Grab a cube or two and add it to sauces and dressings. Use as much or as little as you need.

ESSENTIAL IN: Creamy Pesto Chicken Tortellini (page 64) and Italian Basil-Pesto Chicken (page 26)

QUICK NO-RISE PIZZA DOUGH

We absolutely love pizza, and being able to whip up our own custom pizza at home in the time it takes for delivery is priceless. This dough comes together with no rise time and is perfect to use for pizza, bread sticks, stromboli and calzones. This recipe makes an utterly crisp and chewy crust that is ideal for your favorite toppings. Of course, my crew each has their own idea about what to put on pizza. Chad is a meat lover's pizza guy, Sierra likes just pepperoni and cheese and I love more artisan-style pizzas, such as white pizza with bruschetta topping. When it's homemade, you don't have to compromise: You can have them all. I roll this dough into three small pizzas and have a "top your own pizza" party! Everybody wins . . . and mama gets her white pizza with veggies on top, which is the important part, am I right?

2¼ tsp (9 g) active dry yeast (1 packet)

1 tbsp (12 g) sugar

1½ cups (295 ml) warm water (110°–115°F [43°–46°C])

2 tbsp (30 ml) extra virgin olive oil

3–3½ cups (360–420 g) bread flour (all-purpose will also work), divided

1 tsp kosher salt

In the bowl of a stand mixer fitted with a dough hook, combine the yeast, sugar and warm water. Swirl with a spoon to dissolve the yeast. Let the mixture rest until the yeast becomes foamy and aromatic, about 3 minutes.

Pour the olive oil, 3 cups (360 g) of the flour and the salt into the bowl. Mix on medium speed until the dough comes together in one ball, and then knead for 3 minutes on medium to medium-high speed. The dough should be just a little bit sticky. When you touch your finger to the dough and pull away, you should have just a little dough on your fingertip. Add the remaining flour 1 tablespoon (8 g) at a time as needed. The sticky dough is important to help the pizza crust get a little lift as it cooks.

Lightly flour your countertop. Form the dough into a ball and cover with a dish towel. Let the dough rest for 5 minutes.

Stretch the pizza to your preferred shape and top as desired. I actually use a rolling pin; a professional pizza tosser I am not! Transfer the pizza to a pizza stone or pan and bake the pizza in a preheated 450°F (230°C, or gas mark 8) oven until bubbly and golden brown, 15 to 20 minutes.

If you don't have a stand mixer, see the hand mix method on page 148.

DONNA'S SIMPLE KITCHEN TIP: I love to customize this recipe to create Garlic-Herb Parmesan Pizza Dough. I add 2 teaspoons (6 g) of garlic powder, 1 tablespoon (6 g) of Tuscan-Style Seasoning Blend (page 160) and 1 cup (100 g) of freshly shredded Parmesan cheese. When customizing, add herbs and spices with the oil and add any cheese after the flour.

ESSENTIAL IN: Garlic-Parmesan Pizza Pinwheels (page 78)

SEASONING BLENDS

These seasoning blends are at the top of our list for kitchen essentials because they add so much flavor to recipes. Pretty much everything Italian-inspired that comes out of our kitchen uses the Tuscan-Style Seasoning Blend. It is a glorious blend of aromatic herbs of the classic Italian kitchen. We use it on everything, including omelets and hash browns. The same can be said for the Mexican blend: It is such a spectacular combination of warm and smoky Mexican flavors that we don't even buy taco seasoning anymore; now we use our Mexican Seasoning Blend. It's the fix-all for our picky seven-year-old. I sprinkle it into recipes that she may not normally prefer and voilà, she loves it! Actually, we have pretty much put these seasoning blends on everything; well . . . except oatmeal and ice cream. But there's still time for that.

TUSCAN-STYLE SEASONING BLEND

3 tbsp (9 g) dried rosemary

3 tbsp (9 g) dried oregano

3 tbsp (6 g) dried basil

1½ tbsp (4.5 g) dried thyme

1 tbsp (2 g) dried marjoram

1½ tsp (1 g) dried sage

MEXICAN SEASONING BLEND

4 tbsp (30 g) New Mexico chile powder

2 tbsp (14 g) smoked paprika

2 tbsp (14 g) ground cumin

1 tbsp (9 g) garlic powder

1 tbsp (7 g) onion powder

1 tbsp (3 g) dried oregano leaves

2 tsp (2 g) crushed red pepper flakes

1 tsp cayenne pepper

Combine the ingredients in an airtight 8-ounce (235-ml) mason jar. Seal and shake until well mixed. Store in a cool, dry, dark place.

DONNA'S SIMPLE KITCHEN TIP: For maximum freshness and potency, it is best to store herbs in a sealed airtight container, away from light and heat. Also, moisture can cause caking and other problems, so it's best to avoid keeping them near the stove or in the refrigerator. Replace ground herbs and spices every 6 to 9 months. If the color has faded, most likely so has the flavor. Time to buy fresh ones.

ESSENTIAL IN: Herb-Roasted Italian Vegetables (page 121), Down Home Pot Roast (page 13), Mexican Roast Beef Dip Sandwich (page 25), Home-Style Chicken and Biscuits (page 42)

EIGHT

DELICIOUSLY SIMPLE DESSERTS

When I was growing up, desserts were a special-occasion-only thing in my house. Nowadays, Chad and I like to enjoy a little treat every once in a while. Sierra, on the other hand, thinks that there should be dessert with every meal (maybe she is onto something there). But, reality lies somewhere in between.

When I first started exploring my passion in the kitchen, I began with baking. Oh my word, I could bake for days. I would spend hours upon hours meticulously decorating cookies and assembling decadent seven-layer chocolate desserts that would make your head spin. But after Sierra was born, our priorities changed. Spending hours creating desserts just wasn't my passion anymore. But desserts still are, so now I love creating quick and easy no-bake treats, fun and portable desserts and, of course, our family favorites.

We absolutely love fruit desserts! We could eat berry and lemon treats all day long. Don't get me wrong, though, it's not like I ever met a peanut butter and chocolate dessert that I didn't like. However, we are pretty much known for perfect sugar cookies (page 169). We have been making them for years, and if you ask those who know us, they will most likely reference our sugar cookies that we gift for lots of the holidays. These cookies are probably the only dessert that Chad requests we make again and again. I can't blame him. The cookies are moist and tender, with a slightly crisp edge. And the icing . . . oh my! It dries hard enough to stack, but when you bite into it, it melts in your mouth!

No-Bake Black Bottom Peanut Butter Pie (page 173) has to be one of my favorite desserts. It is certainly my favorite pie. The cookie crust and rich and creamy peanut butter filling are enough to make me break out in the happy dance!

Strawberry Cheesecake No-Bake Ice Box Cake (page 165) is Sierra's favorite dessert. We all love sweet, juicy strawberries, and combined with the rich and creamy cheesecake filling, this one hits it out of the park!

Okay, I have to admit I made the No-Bake Rocky Road Avalanche Bars (page 166) at least twelve times while we were writing this book. Luckily, our friends and family were all willing to share them with us. They are so amazing. Creamy peanut butter and chocolate combine with crisp rice cereal and fluffy marshmallows (swoon). They make me go weak in the knees.

Life is too short . . . forget the fork and just dig in!

STRAWBERRY CHEESECAKE NO-BAKE ICE BOX CAKE

Layer upon layer of blissfully creamy strawberry cheesecake and fluffy vanilla whipped cream flecked with chunks of juicy sweet strawberries and graham crackers in a no-bake dessert is like a dream come true. We could eat this for days, and Sierra goes crazy over it! It's a no-fuss recipe, and all of the magic happens in the freezer. That's our kind of dessert!

1 lb (454 g) strawberries, hulled, divided

4 cups (940 ml) heavy cream

¾ cup (150 g) sugar, divided

2 tbsp (30 ml) vanilla extract

8 oz (227 g) cream cheese, softened

16 graham cracker sheets

1 tbsp (9 g) dry instant vanilla pudding mix

DONNA'S SIMPLE KITCHEN TIP: Run your knife under hot water to warm the knife. Dry the knife, and then cut the cake. The knife should slide through the cake more easily. Repeat as necessary.

Generously line a 9 x 5-inch (23 x 12.7-cm) loaf pan with plastic wrap. Make sure there is enough hanging over the sides to wrap across the top.

Finely chop half of the strawberries in the blender and set them aside. Chop the remaining strawberries into bite-size pieces. (I cut each strawberry into about 8 pieces.)

In a tall mixing bowl, combine the heavy cream, ½ cup (100 g) of the sugar and the vanilla with an electric mixer. Whip until stiff peaks form. Divide the whipped cream evenly into 2 bowls. Pop one in the refrigerator to use for the frosting. We'll use the other bowl for the cake.

Beat the cream cheese and the remaining ¼ cup (50 g) of sugar in a large bowl with an electric mixer until fluffy, about 3 minutes. Fold about half of the whipped cream (for the cake) and all of the finely chopped strawberries into the cream cheese mixture until completely combined. Set aside.

Add one-third of the remaining whipped cream to the pan (this isn't math class; just eyeball it) and spread it into an even layer. Top with a layer of graham crackers, breaking them up to make them fit if you need to. Then add half of the cheesecake mixture to the pan in an even layer and top with a second layer of graham crackers.

Stir half of the bite-size strawberries into the remaining whipped cream for the cake (refrigerate the remaining strawberries until ready to use) and pour the whipped cream into the pan in an even layer. Top with a third layer of graham crackers and spread the remaining cheesecake mixture in an even layer on top; top with the fourth and final layer of graham crackers. Pull the excess plastic wrap across the top and freeze the cake for 2 to 3 hours or refrigerate for 4 to 6 hours.

Remove the cake from the freezer, uncover the plastic wrap and invert the cake onto a plate. Remove the plastic wrap. Whisk the instant pudding mix into the reserved whipped cream (for the frosting) to stabilize it. If the whipped cream loses its fluffiness, you can beat it with the mixer again until stiff peaks form. Frost the cake with the whipped cream and decorate the top with the remaining bite-size strawberries.

NO-BAKE ROCKY ROAD AVALANCHE BARS

With the perfect balance of chocolate and peanut butter, these no-bake bars are utterly addictive. Soft, billowy marshmallows and crispy rice cereal come together with the rich and creamy chocolate peanut butter candy filling to create this memorable dessert. No-fuss desserts are our thing, and as much as we love sharing them with our family and friends, we sometimes have to make extra because we can't keep our hands off them! These No-Bake Rocky Road Avalanche Bars are so good I am in the kitchen doing my happy dance. Chocolate and peanut butter with a candy crunch? Sign me up, twice!

1 lb (454 g) chocolate-flavored candy coating (I use Plymouth Pantry's almond bark or Candiquik)

2 cups (350 g) semisweet chocolate chips

4 oz (112 g) German's sweet chocolate bar, broken into chunks

1 (16.9-oz [473-g]) jar super chunky peanut butter

3 cups (64 g) crispy rice cereal

3 cups (150 g) mini marshmallows

½ tsp salt

Line a 9 x 13-inch (23 x 33-cm) baking pan with parchment paper.

Melt the chocolate candy coating, chocolate chips and German chocolate in a large heatproof bowl. Microwave at half power for 30 seconds at a time until melted and smooth, stirring after each interval. Stir the peanut butter into the warm chocolate until melted and smooth. Add the rice cereal, marshmallows and salt and stir to combine.

Pour the mixture into the prepared pan. Allow it to set in a cool place until firm. You can refrigerate the pan if your kitchen is too warm, or, if you are impatient like me, pop them in the freezer for 20 minutes. Once they are solid, cut them into 24 pieces.

DONNA'S SIMPLE KITCHEN TIP: You can also use aluminum foil sprayed with nonstick cooking spray to line your pan.

DONNA'S FAMOUS SUGAR COOKIES

This perfect sugar cookie is soft and tender on the inside and slightly crisp on the outside. It's bursting with flavor from the vanilla and almond extracts. The no-chill dough means cookie-making is that much more fun. Our local bakery told us years ago that the trick to cut-out cookies keeping their shape was to skip the leavening. Now they are perfect every time.

Chad and I were married in a dreamy winter wonderland wedding, complete with a cookie and cocoa bar for our guests to enjoy. That was the year that we started making these amazing sugar cookies and everyone goes crazy over them. The cookie alone is absolutely amazing, but the icing puts them over the top!

8 tbsp (112 g) unsalted butter, softened

1 cup (200 g) granulated sugar

1 large egg, at room temperature

1 tsp vanilla extract

½ tsp almond extract

2–2½ cups (240–300 g) all-purpose flour

¼ tsp kosher salt

1 recipe Best-Tasting Sugar Cookie Icing (optional, page 170)

Preheat the oven to 375°F (190°C, or gas mark 5). Line 2 baking sheets with parchment paper or silicone baking mats.

Cream the butter and sugar in the bowl of an electric mixer on medium speed until light and fluffy, 3 to 5 minutes. Add the egg and extracts and beat until the batter is well-mixed. Add the flour and the salt and mix on low speed until just combined. Do not overmix. The dough should be tacky, not sticky, when you take it out of the bowl. If it is sticky, add a little flour and mix it in. Depending on the weather and ingredients, it may take anywhere from 2 to 2½ cups (240 to 300 g) of flour.

Roll the dough out on a lightly floured countertop or on a floured silicone mat. We like our cookies ¼ to ⅜-inch (6 to 9-mm) thick. Cut the dough with cookie cutters and place the cookies on the baking sheet. If you would like to add sprinkles, now is the time.

Bake for 9 to 11 minutes, until the cookies are slightly golden around the edges. If you are baking 2 pans at the same time, be sure to rotate the pans halfway through the baking time. Remove the cookies from the oven and allow them to cool for 5 minutes on the baking sheet. Use a spatula to transfer the cookies to a cooling rack to continue cooling completely. Decorate as desired.

DONNA'S SIMPLE KITCHEN TIPS: We got this brilliant tip for shipping cookies from our friend who owns a cookie shop, and it works so well. Package the cookies individually and tape them to a piece of cardboard. Wrap the cardboard in bubble wrap. You can stack multiple layers of cookies.

If you are sensitive to almond, you can use all vanilla extract.

BEST-TASTING SUGAR COOKIE ICING

This four-ingredient recipe is the best-tasting icing we have ever had. It is crisp when you bite into it, but then it immediately starts melting in your mouth. It kind of tastes like marshmallow with a flavor that you just can't put your finger on. Our secret ingredient? Almond extract. It gives the cookies that "Wow! What the heck is in these?" flavor. We have been making this icing for more than ten years and everyone goes crazy over it. Chad and I once made 600 cookies for a charity event and everyone who bought a cookie raved about them. Luckily, the icing dries hard enough to pack and ship, so transporting them is a breeze.

Decorating is so much fun. We make a bunch of colors and put them into decorator squeeze bottles and put out a bunch of sprinkles or dragées and the whole family decorates together. Sierra is getting to be an amazing cookie decorator. Can you spot her cookie? Hint: It's the pretty yellow one at the top. Beautiful icing that dries to a gorgeous sheen and tastes amazing? Yep, it's bowl-licking good. Not that I would know anything about that. {wink}

3 cups (360 g) powdered sugar

2–4 tbsp (30–60 ml) whole milk, divided

2 tbsp (30 ml) light corn syrup

1 tsp almond extract (or your favorite flavor)

Gel food coloring (in desired colors)

In a large bowl, combine the sugar and 2 tablespoons (30 ml) of the milk. Mix with an electric mixer until it's completely smooth. Add more of the remaining 2 tablespoons (30 ml) of milk if you need to, 1 tablespoon (15 ml) at a time. Add the corn syrup and almond extract. Stir until combined. Divide the icing among the number of bowls needed for decorating, or use as is.

Add food coloring, one drop at a time, until the desired color is reached. Pour the icing into squeeze bottles, decorator bags or cups. Keep the unused icing sealed until ready to use. If you are leaving it in the bowl, be sure to cover it with plastic wrap or the sugar will harden on the top. Decorate your cookies and allow them to dry overnight or enjoy immediately. I keep them on a cookie sheet tented with foil while drying.

DONNA'S SIMPLE KITCHEN TIPS: Your outline icing should be the consistency of toothpaste. Flood icing should be the consistency of corn syrup. To get the two consistencies, start with thick outline icing. Divide the icing among bowls to color. For example, if you are making blue, color the bowl of icing, then pour your outline icing into the squeeze bottle and thin the remaining icing with a little milk (or water). Add a few drops at a time until it is the consistency of corn syrup. When I am shortcutting, I just make one icing that is thick and I microwave the bottle for a few seconds when I need to thin it out. You could also warm the squeeze bottle in a bowl of warm water.

The decorator squeeze bottles are my favorite. You can pick them up in the cake decorating section at your local craft store.

If you are sensitive to almond, you can use vanilla extract, but it will give your icing an off-white color. If you are going to color it, you will not notice.

NO-BAKE BLACK BOTTOM PEANUT BUTTER PIE

This dreamy pie starts with a rich and creamy peanut butter filling with bits of peanut speckled throughout. It is set atop a black bottom cookie crust, topped with homemade whipped cream and finished with peanut butter cups, roasted peanuts and a sweet chocolate drizzle! This sweet treat takes me back to a little diner in Florida, where I first fell in love . . . with peanut butter pie. Just me, a fork and that amazing pie. {swoon} Isn't life grand?

24 Oreo cookies

5 tbsp (70 g) unsalted butter, melted

3⅛ cups (735 ml) heavy cream, divided

2¼ cups (270 g) powdered sugar, divided

1½ cups (390 g) chunky peanut butter

12 oz (340 g) cream cheese, softened

¼ cup (45 g) semisweet chocolate

10 mini Reese's Peanut Butter Cups, quartered

¼ cup (35 g) honey-roasted peanuts, chopped

Place the cookies into your food processor and pulse until they look like fine crumbs. Slowly pour the butter in through the feed tube and pulse until the crumbs are completely coated in the butter. Pour the crumbs into a 9-inch (23-cm) deep-dish pie plate and press the mixture onto the bottom and up the sides to form the pie crust. Put the pie crust in the freezer while you make the filling.

In a tall mixing bowl, whip 3 cups (705 ml) of the heavy cream and ¾ cup (90 g) of the powdered sugar with an electric mixer until stiff peaks form. Put the whipped cream in the refrigerator while you start the filling.

In a large bowl, beat the peanut butter, cream cheese and remaining 1½ cups (180 g) of powdered sugar with an electric mixer until light and fluffy, about 3 minutes. Fold in half (just eyeball it) of the whipped cream until it is completely incorporated. Scoop the filling into the chilled pie crust and smooth into an even layer. Dollop the remaining whipped cream over the top and use a spatula to smooth it into an even layer. Put the pie in the refrigerator while you prepare the toppings.

Combine the chocolate and the remaining ⅛ cup (30 ml) of heavy cream in a small microwave-safe mixing bowl. Microwave for 45 seconds, let the chocolate sit for 5 minutes to let the chocolate melt into the cream completely and then stir until well-combined.

Sprinkle the peanut butter cups and peanuts over the top of the pie. Drizzle the chocolate ganache over the top. Serve immediately or refrigerate for 4 hours to let the pie completely set up.

DONNA'S SIMPLE KITCHEN TIP: For a gorgeous drizzle, transfer the chocolate to a plastic sandwich bag and twist the bag closed, forcing out all the air. Cut off a corner of the bag (the smaller the hole, the smaller the drizzle will be) and squeeze it out to create a gorgeous drizzle.

KEY LIME NO-BAKE ICE BOX CAKE

This rich and creamy no-bake treat is perfectly tart with just the right amount of sweetness. Graham crackers are sandwiched between the tangy filling, and the icing on the cake, literally, is the marshmallow whipped cream. It is truly magical! In Florida, where I grew up, citrus was so abundant that fruit pies were at every get-together and Key lime pie was a go-to dessert. We absolutely adore citrus. As a matter of fact, we would take a citrus dessert over chocolate any day of the week. This old classic transformed into a no-fuss ice box cake is glorious and purely refreshing. Key lime pie has never tasted so good!

8 oz (227 g) cream cheese, softened

1¼ cups (150 g) powdered sugar

2 cups (470 ml) heavy cream, divided

1 tbsp (6 g) Key lime zest

2 tbsp (28 g) unsalted butter, at room temperature

½ tsp salt

½ cup (120 ml) Key lime juice

16 whole graham crackers

1 cup (120 g) marshmallow crème

Generously line a 9 x 5-inch (23 x 12.7-cm) loaf pan with plastic wrap. Make sure there is enough hanging over the sides to wrap across the top.

In a tall mixing bowl, beat the cream cheese and powdered sugar with an electric mixer until smooth. With the mixer on low speed, slowly add 1 cup (235 ml) of the heavy cream. Do not add it all at once or the filling will become lumpy. With the mixer on medium speed, whip the mixture until stiff peaks form.

Save a pinch of lime zest for topping the cake. Add the remaining zest, butter and the salt to your cream cheese mixture. With the mixer on low speed, slowly pour in the lime juice. Once the mixture is fully combined, set aside.

Spread about 1 cup (150 g) of filling in the bottom of the loaf pan. Use a spatula to spread it evenly. Top the filling with a layer of graham crackers, breaking them if necessary to make them fit (save all those broken pieces, because we will be using them for the top of the cake). Repeat the filling and the graham cracker layers 3 more times, until you have 4 layers of filling and 4 layers of graham crackers, ending with graham crackers. Cover with the plastic wrap and freeze for 2 to 3 hours.

Add the remaining 1 cup (235 ml) heavy cream to a tall bowl and beat with an electric mixer on medium speed until medium peaks form. Add the marshmallow crème and beat until combined. Don't worry if the cream looks a little lumpy; the marshmallow will melt into the whipped cream as the cake sets up.

Remove the cake from the freezer, uncover the plastic wrap and invert the pan onto a plate. Remove the plastic wrap from the cake. Frost the cake with the marshmallow whipped cream and sprinkle the top with the reserved graham cracker bits and lime zest. Refrigerate until ready to serve.

DONNA'S SIMPLE KITCHEN TIP: Roll your limes on the counter while applying pressure with your palm. It will warm up the lime and loosen the cells that hold the juice, so you get more juice.

LEGENDARY
PECAN PIE BARS

Imagine a soft and tender brown sugar–vanilla bean shortbread cookie crust with a buttery pecan caramel topping all in a portable pecan pie bar. Oh my heavens, it makes me weak in the knees to think about it. Who knew that a pecan dessert recipe that my mom shared with me so many years ago would evolve into this passion that I have for cooking and baking? This recipe has been a labor of love in memory of my mom. My pecan bars were her absolute favorite recipe, and for good reason. I mean, look at all of those toasted pecans covered in that scrumptious caramel filling. Notice the ratio of topping to crust? Oh, yeah! What can I say about the dessert that started it all? Well, as our seven-year-old Sierra says, "If one bite isn't enough to make you want to eat the whole pan, then your 'taste bugs' must be broken."

2 cups (4 sticks [450 g]) unsalted butter, at room temperature, divided

2 cups (450 g) packed light brown sugar, divided

2 tbsp (20 g) vanilla bean paste, divided

2 cups (240 g) all-purpose flour

½ cup (120 ml) light corn syrup

¼ cup (60 ml) heavy cream

1 lb (454 g) raw pecans, chopped

DONNA'S SIMPLE KITCHEN TIPS:

I highly recommend finding a really good vanilla bean paste. It is concentrated vanilla in a thick paste loaded with vanilla bean seeds. I use it in everything from pancakes and waffles to whipped cream and desserts. It is sooo good. Still, you can substitute pure vanilla extract.

You can substitute honey for the corn syrup. The bars are delightful either way.

Preheat the oven to 350°F (180°C, or gas mark 4). Line a 9 x 13-inch (23 x 33-cm) pan with parchment paper for easy bar removal.

In a large bowl using a hand mixer, cream 1 cup (225 g) of the butter and ½ cup (112 g) of the brown sugar until light and fluffy, about 3 minutes. Add 1 tablespoon (10 g) of the vanilla bean paste and mix until combined. With the mixer on low speed, add the flour and mix until the flour and butter have come together.

Scoop the dough into the pan. Use your fingertips to press the dough evenly into the pan. It may fight you at first. Stick with it (no pun intended) and it will come together. Bake for 15 minutes, until the crust is lightly browned around the edges. Allow the crust to cool in the refrigerator (or freezer) while you prepare the filling, but leave the oven on.

In a 4-quart (3.6-L) saucepan over medium-high heat, combine the remaining 1 cup (225 g) of butter, the remaining 1½ cups (338 g) of brown sugar and the corn syrup. Stir until well-blended. Bring to a boil and stir frequently for 3 minutes. The mixture will get light and airy. Remove the pan from the heat and add the heavy cream and the remaining 1 tablespoon (10 g) of vanilla bean paste. Stir until combined. Add the pecans and stir until they are completely coated.

Remove the shortbread crust from the refrigerator (or freezer) and pour the topping over the crust, using a spatula to spread it into an even layer. Return the pan to the oven and bake for 25 minutes, until the pecan topping is set (it will move slowly when you jiggle the pan). Allow the bars to cool completely before cutting to get those beautiful straight lines, or if you are impatient like me, eat them as soon as they are cool enough to put in your mouth.

BERRY BANANA CHEESECAKE SALAD

Rich and creamy no-bake cheesecake filling is folded into luscious berries and sweet bananas to create the most amazing, glorious fruit salad ever! Again, no-bake desserts rule in our simple kitchen, and this one is an excellent example. It's sweet, fresh and the perfect crowd-pleasing potluck dessert. Fresh berries and cheesecake—what's not to love?

8 oz (227 g) cream cheese, softened

½ cup (60 g) powdered sugar

1 cup (235 ml) heavy cream

1 tsp vanilla bean paste

1 lb (454 g) fresh strawberries, hulled and sliced

9 oz (252 g) fresh blueberries

3 medium bananas, cut into coins

2 tbsp (30 ml) fresh lemon juice

In a medium bowl using an electric mixer, beat the cream cheese and sugar until smooth, about 3 minutes. It may bind up in the beaters, but stick with it and it will loosen up.

With the mixer on low speed, slowly add the heavy cream about 1 tablespoon (15 ml) at a time, mixing until smooth and all of the cream has combined into the cream cheese. Don't add it all at once—trust me on this one. Add the vanilla and beat the cheesecake mixture until it is thick and fluffy. Place the cheesecake mixture in the refrigerator while you prep the fruit.

In a large bowl, combine the sliced strawberries, blueberries, banana coins and lemon juice. Stir until all the fruit is coated with lemon juice. Gently fold the cheesecake mixture into the fruit until combined. Serve immediately or chill the cheesecake salad until ready to serve.

DONNA'S SIMPLE KITCHEN TIP: Toss bananas in lemon juice to keep them from browning.

OVERNIGHT CINNAMON ROLLS

A sweetened roll with a thick cinnamon-sugar filling and a luscious, rich cream cheese frosting could be the perfect dessert or breakfast, but this overnight recipe makes these a home run! When I first met Chad, he brought me to the "house of cinnamon rolls." I had never seen a breakfast pastry quite so big or tasted one so delicious! Over the years, I have worked on many cinnamon roll recipes, and this one will knock your socks off. I am not a morning person, so the thought of preparing cinnamon rolls in the a.m. makes it a no-go, but these cinnamon rolls can be made the night before and popped into the oven in the morning . . . Oh yeah, now we *are* the house of cinnamon rolls!

ROLLS

Flour, for dusting

1 recipe 40-Minute Milk and Honey Dinner Rolls (page 148), unbaked

1 cup (225 g) packed light brown sugar

2 tbsp (14 g) ground cinnamon

1 tsp cornstarch

4 tbsp (56 g) unsalted butter, softened

FROSTING

4 oz (112 g) cream cheese, softened

4 tbsp (56 g) unsalted butter, softened

1 cup (120 g) powdered sugar

½ tbsp (7.5 ml) fresh lemon juice

1 tsp vanilla extract

¼ tsp kosher salt

DONNA'S SIMPLE KITCHEN TIP:
When covering dough, spray the underside of the plastic wrap to keep it from sticking. Lay the cut plastic wrap on the countertop and spray it with nonstick spray. Place the plastic wrap on the dough, sprayed side facing the dough.

To make the rolls, lightly dust the countertop with flour. Turn the dinner roll dough out onto the countertop. Shape the dough into a ball and allow it to rest for 5 minutes. Meanwhile, combine the light brown sugar, cinnamon and cornstarch in a medium bowl and stir with a fork until combined.

Knead the dough a few turns, and then use a rolling pin to roll out the dough into a 12 x 18-inch (30.5 x 46-cm) rectangle. Use your fingertips to spread the softened butter around the dough, leaving a 1-inch (2.5-cm) border along the bottom uncoated. Sprinkle the brown sugar mixture over the butter, again leaving the bottom 1 inch (2.5 cm) uncoated. Use a rolling pin to gently roll across the sugar mixture to press it into the dough, so it doesn't fall out as you roll it.

Starting at the top, tightly roll the dough toward you, using the last 1 inch (2.5 cm) to seal the roll. Cut the dough roll in half to create 2 logs and then cut those halves into thirds. You will have 6 pieces. Again, math is amazing.

Grease a 9 x 13-inch (23 x 33-cm) baking dish with butter. Evenly space the rolls in the baking dish, 2 rows of 3 rolls in each, placing the end pieces upside down. Loosely cover the baking pan with a piece of plastic wrap sprayed on the underside with nonstick spray and place it in the refrigerator overnight.

Preheat the oven to 350°F (180°C, or gas mark 4). Remove the rolls from the refrigerator and let them sit out in a warm part of your kitchen for 30 minutes to take the chill off. Bake for 25 to 30 minutes, until golden brown and cooked through.

To make the frosting, in a medium mixing bowl with an electric mixer, beat the cream cheese, butter and powdered sugar until light and fluffy, about 3 minutes. Add the lemon juice, vanilla and salt and beat until combined.

Remove the rolls from the oven and spread half of the frosting over the warm rolls. Let the rolls cool slightly and spread the rest of the frosting on the rolls.

CRAZY CARAMEL APPLE PIE BOMBS

After enjoying this fun twist on the classic apple pie, you may never go back! A tender, buttery sweet bread is stuffed with juicy tart apples in a creamy caramel sauce and baked to perfection. When you bite into one of these heavenly dessert bombs, a river of sweet caramel runs over them, making this a perfectly satisfying, sweet portable treat. Before Sierra was born (actually, the year I was pregnant with her), Chad's mom taught us how to prepare a special family recipe that we have now been making together for years. Sierra even gets in on the action and helps. That recipe starts with stuffing bread dough, and it inspired the invention of all of the scrumptious bomb recipes that we have made. These explode with flavor and are loaded with ooey-gooey deliciousness.

4 tbsp (56 g) unsalted butter, melted, divided

2 medium apples, such as Granny Smith or Honeycrisp, peeled, cored and diced

6 tbsp (90 g) packed light brown sugar, divided

1 tbsp (7 g) ground cinnamon

30 caramels, divided

All-purpose flour, for dusting

1 recipe 40-Minute Milk and Honey Dinner Rolls (page 148), unbaked

2 tbsp (30 ml) heavy cream

Preheat the oven to 350°F (180°C, or gas mark 4). Butter an 8 x 8-inch (20 x 20-cm) baking pan with 2 tablespoons (28 g) of the butter and set aside.

Combine the apples, 2 tablespoons (30 g) of the brown sugar and the cinnamon in a medium bowl and toss to coat. Set aside. Unwrap the caramels and cut 18 of them into quarters. Set aside. Lightly flour your countertop.

Flatten each dough ball into a circle about 3 inches (7.5 cm) across. You can use a rolling pin or you can pull the dough around the edges like you are making a mini pizza. Add 1 tablespoon (10 g) of the apple mixture and 6 of the cut caramel pieces. Carefully pull each side over the center to create a "package," and then roll the dough into a ball. Be careful to make sure you cannot see through the dough. If you have any tears or can't seal the dough, tap your fingertips in flour, pinch any tears and roll again.

Place the dough ball in the prepared dish, seam side down. Repeat until all of the apple pie bombs are in the dish. Brush the apple pie bombs with the remaining 2 tablespoons (28 g) of melted butter and sprinkle with the remaining 4 tablespoons (60 g) of brown sugar. Bake the bombs for 30 to 35 minutes, until the tops are golden brown and they are no longer doughy.

Meanwhile, place the remaining 12 caramels and the heavy cream in a microwave-safe bowl and microwave until melted, 30 seconds at a time, stirring after each interval. Once you have a smooth mixture, set aside to cool.

Remove the apple pie bombs from the oven and drizzle with the caramel sauce.

DONNA'S SIMPLE KITCHEN TIPS: If any of the delicious caramel escapes during cooking, scoop it up and spoon it over the top as a sauce.

You can use frozen yeast dinner-roll balls in place of the homemade dough.

OOEY-GOOEY FUDGY CHOCOLATE BROWNIES

These brownies are rich, chocolaty and melt-in-your-mouth delicious. Brownies are absolutely the number one dessert coming out of our kitchen. We make more of them than any other dessert, and more often than not, they are headed over to my in-laws' house. And believe me, Gigi and Pop Pop are always happy to receive them! Well, when it's just one bowl and 30 minutes until you can have brownies, why wouldn't you make them for everyone? After all, more brownie gifts to the grandparents do mean more free date-night babysitting, am I right?

2 cups (350 g) semisweet chocolate chips

1 cup (120 g) all-purpose flour, divided

1 cup (2 sticks [225 g]) butter

1 tsp instant coffee granules

1½ cups (300 g) granulated sugar

1 cup (225 g) packed light brown sugar

1 cup (120 g) unsweetened cocoa powder

1 tbsp (10 g) vanilla bean paste

4 large eggs

½ tsp baking powder

½ tsp salt

Preheat the oven to 350°F (180°C, or gas mark 4). Line a 9 x 13-inch (23 x 33-cm) baking pan with parchment paper for easy cleanup. It will also make pulling the brownies out of the pan a cinch. Set the pan aside.

Combine the chocolate chips and ¼ cup (30 g) of the flour in a small bowl. Mix them to coat the chocolate and set aside.

Place the butter in a large microwave-safe mixing bowl and heat, about 30 seconds at a time, until melted, stirring between each interval. Sprinkle the coffee granules over the warm butter and stir until mostly dissolved. Add the sugars, cocoa powder, vanilla bean paste, eggs, baking powder and salt. Beat on medium-high speed with an electric mixer until well-combined, about 3 minutes. This step is whipping the eggs and sugar very well to help create that crinkly "meringue-ish" top.

Add the remaining ¾ cup (90 g) of flour. Mix just until the flour is completely combined and there are no visible white spots in the brownie batter. Sprinkle the floured chocolate chips, including any flour that has sunk to the bottom, over the top of the batter and fold in the chips with a spatula.

Pour the brownie batter into the prepared baking pan. Bake for 25 minutes, or until the brownies have risen and are cooked through. Allow to cool completely before cutting.

DONNA'S SIMPLE KITCHEN TIP: For perfectly cut brownies, even when they are hot, use a disposable plastic knife.

See our tip on vanilla bean paste on page 177.

THANKS!

First of all, we thank God every day, for without Him, none of this would be possible.

To our family and friends, we are so grateful for your love and support during this amazing journey, especially those of you who could make it to our house in 15 minutes flat when we had recipes to test.

And to Page Street Publishing, and in particular Will, Marissa and Meg, for believing in us and helping us bring our vision of *The Simple Kitchen* to reality.

To my mom, for teaching me that the kitchen is a fun place to be, for sharing that one recipe with me that would shape our destiny and our future, for a family legacy filled with great memories and contagious laughter, and most importantly, for an unending supply of butter.

To Chad's mom and bonus dad (Gigi and Pop Pop), for inviting us into your kitchen to share family traditions that we will cherish forever. We are so grateful to be able to share our stories, our experiences and our food with you . . . lots and lots of food. Especially brownies.

To my dad and Carolyn, for always believing in us. And Dad, thank you for the ride to the airport to meet my destiny so many years ago and the money to get back, in case it didn't work out.

To Chad's dad and Roseanne, for encouraging us to write a cookbook for so many years, for helping us eat our way through Houston and for waiting in line for three hours for some "pretty good" barbecue.

To Brad (Uncle Happy), we are so grateful for your lifelong friendship, honest opinions and long conversations. Most of all, we thank you for being the #1 world champion fried chicken taste tester.

To all of our loyal readers, for helping make the journey more fun than the destination, and for all of the food, fun and laughter. We thank you for sharing your days with us, and for sharing your photos, your stories and your support. And no, we still can't deliver dinner to your house.

And to our Sierra, without whom our days would be boring! You are the wind in our sails and the best part of our family snuggles at the end of the day. You are Mommy's mini-me and forever Daddy's little girl. Side by side, every day is more amazing because you are in it . . . and messier—much, much messier.

FROM DONNA: To Chad, for being my partner on this amazing journey of ours, for eating all of the delicious food and some not-so-tasty food, for the countless trips to the grocery store without fussing too much, for always making the food look as good as it tastes (if not better), for taste-testing seven versions of Everything Cheese Sauce and for always staying grounded, so I can fly. I love you, forever. Most of all, I thank you for chasing me down in that Yahoo! chat room so many years ago.

FROM CHAD: To Donna, my wonderful wife, thank you for being the best friend, wife and business partner that anyone could have ever asked for. This journey we are on is amazing and I couldn't imagine doing it with anyone else. You inspire me to be the best that I can be in everything I do and for that I am forever grateful. You are my other half, my best friend and the love of my life. Thank you for always being the best woman I have ever known. I love you.

ABOUT THE AUTHORS

Donna and Chad Elick are the creators of the hugely popular website The Slow Roasted Italian, created in 2011, where millions of readers come every month in search of time-saving recipes. Since then, they have developed and photographed more than 1,000 recipes.

Donna is an author and recipe developer. She is a busy wife and mom with a passion for creating quick and easy meals that are bursting with flavor and made with as many real ingredients as possible. She is a self-taught cook who grew up on the sandy beaches in a little town in southwest Florida and found her husband and a love for bold flavors in Phoenix, Arizona. When Donna is not in the kitchen cooking, she loves gardening, party planning, traveling and spending time at home with Chad and their daughter.

Chad is the photographer, food stylist, graphic designer and chief taste tester. He studied graphic design in college and worked as an art director for twenty years. Luckily, he picked up a camera and taught himself to take the most mouthwatering photography. Chad can usually be found with camera in hand, taking a walk with their daughter, on long bike rides, or researching and playing with the latest tech. Mostly, Chad spends his time coming up with innovative ideas to solve Donna's problems.

They currently live in Phoenix, Arizona, with their daughter, Sierra, and an endless supply of nachos.

Connect with Donna and Chad: TheSlowRoastedItalian.com

Facebook	Pinterest	Instagram	Twitter
@slowroasted	@slowroasted	@slowroasted	@slow_roasted

INDEX